FAITH in AMERICA

FAITH
in AMERICA

The Powerful Impact of One Company Speaking Out Boldly

STEVE GREEN

President of **HOBBY LOBBY**

LOOKING GLASS BOOKS

Faith in America

Published by Looking Glass Books, Inc.
Decatur, Georgia

Copyright © 2011 by Steve Green

Book and jacket design by Burtch Hunter Design

ISBN 978-1-929619-43-6

Manufactured in Canada

To my parents, David and Barbara Green,
who faithfully passed on to me the love of
Jesus Christ that they were given by their parents.
Their hard work and sacrifice have made this book possible.

CONTENTS

FAITH
in AMERICA

In God We Trust

Presidents

"It is the duty of all nations to acknowledge the providence of Almighty God, to obey His will, to be grateful for His benefits, and humbly to implore His protection and favor."

GEORGE WASHINGTON
Commander-in-Chief in the American Revolution; Signer of the Constitution;
First President of the United States

"We have no government armed with power capable of contending with human passions unbridled by morality and religion. Our Constitution was made only for a moral and religious people. It is wholly inadequate to the government of any other."

JOHN ADAMS
Signer of the Declaration of Independence; One of Two Signers of the Bill of Rights;
Second President of the United States

"Before any man can be considered as a member of civil society, he must be considered as a subject of the Governor of the Universe.

JAMES MADISON
Signer of the Constitution; Fourth President of the United States

"And can the liberties of a nation be thought secure when we have removed their only firm basis, a conviction in the minds of the people that these liberties are of the gift of God? That they are not to be violated but with His wrath? Indeed I tremble for my country when I reflect that God is just; that His justice cannot sleep forever."

THOMAS JEFFERSON
Signer and the principal author of the Declaration of Independence;
Third President of the United States

"Is it not that in the chain of human events, the birthday of the nation is indissolubly linked with the birthday of the Savior? – that it forms a leading event in the progress of the Gospel dispensation? Is it not that the Declaration of Independence first organized the social compact on the foundation of the Redeemer's mission upon earth? – that it laid the cornerstone of human government upon the first precepts of Christianity?"

JOHN QUINCY ADAMS
Statesman; Diplomat; Sixth President of the United States

Founding Fathers

"An appeal to arms and to the God of hosts is all that is left us!...Sir, we are not weak if we make a proper use of those means which the God of nature hath placed in our power... Besides, sir, we shall not fight our battles alone. There is a just God who presides over the destinies of nations and who will raise up friends to fight our battles for us...Is life so dear, or peace so sweet as to be purchased at the price of chains and slavery? Forbid it, Almighty God! I know not what course others may take; but as for me, give me liberty or give me death!!!"

PATRICK HENRY
Patriot and Statesman

"To the kindly influence of Christianity we owe that degree of civil freedom, and political and social happiness, which mankind now enjoys...Whenever the pillars of Christianity shall be overthrown, our present republican forms of government – and all blessings which flow from them – must fall with them."

JEDEDIAH MORSE
Patriot and Educator, called "The Father of American Geography"

"I've lived, sir, a long time, and the longer I live, the more convincing proofs I see of this truth: That God governs in the affairs of men. If a sparrow cannot fall to the ground without His notice, is it probable that an empire can rise without His aid? We've been assured in the sacred writings that unless the Lord builds the house, they labor in vain who build it. I firmly believe this, and I also believe that without His concurring aid, we shall succeed in this political building no better than the builders of Babel."

BENJAMIN FRANKLIN
Signer of the Declaration of Independence and the Constitution

Supreme Court Justices

The Bible is the best of all books, for it is the word of God and teaches us the way to be happy in this world and in the next. Continue therefore to read it and to regulate your life by its precepts.

Providence has given to our people the choice of their rulers, and it is the duty, as well as the privilege and interest of our Christian nation, to select and prefer Christians for their rulers.

JOHN JAY
Co-author of the Federalist Papers; First Chief-Justice of the U.S. Supreme Court

Human law must rest its authority ultimately upon the authority of that law which is Divine. ... Far from being rivals or enemies, religion and law are twin sisters, friends, and mutual assistants. Indeed, these two sciences run into each other.

JAMES WILSON
Signer of both the Declaration of Independence and the Constitution;
Original Justice on the U.S. Supreme Court

One of the beautiful boasts of our municipal jurisprudence is that Christianity is a part of the Common Law...There never has been a period in which the Common Law did not recognize Christianity as lying at its foundations...I verily believe Christianity necessary to the support of civil society.

JOSEPH STORY
U.S. Supreme Court Justice, "Father of American Jurisprudence," Placed on the
Court by President James Madison

Congress

"We are a Christian people...not because the law demands it, not to gain exclusive benefits or to avoid legal disabilities, but from choice and education; and in a land thus universally Christian, what is to be expected, what desired, but that we shall pay due regard to Christianity?"

[Senate Judiciary Committee Report, January 19, 1853]

"At the time of the adoption of the Constitution and the amendments, the universal sentiment was that Christianity should be encouraged...In this age there can be no substitute for Christianity...That was the religion of the founders of the republic and they expected it to remain the religion of their descendants."

[House Judiciary Committee Report, March 27, 1854]

Education

"Let every student be plainly instructed and earnestly pressed to consider well the main end of his life and studies is to know God and Jesus Christ which is eternal life (John 17.3) and therefore to lay Christ in the bottom as the only foundation of all sound knowledge and learning. And seeing the Lord only giveth wisdom, let every one seriously set himself by prayer in secret to seek it of Him (Proverbs 2, 3). Every one shall so exercise himself in reading the Scriptures twice a day that he shall be ready to give such an account of his proficiency therein."

HARVARD
1636 Student Guidelines

"All the scholars are required to live a religious and blameless life according to the rules of God's Word, diligently reading the Holy Scriptures, that fountain of Divine light and truth, and constantly attending all the duties of religion."

YALE
1787 Student Guidelines

Supreme Court Rulings

There is no dissonance in these [legal] declarations...These are not individual sayings, declarations of private persons: they are organic [legal, governmental] utterances; they speak the voice of the entire people...These, and many other matters which might be noticed, add a volume of unofficial declarations to the mass of organic utterances that this is a Christian nation.

Church of the Holy Trinity v. U.S. 1892
Unanimous Decision Declaring America a Christian Nation
Significantly, the U.S. Supreme Court cited dozens of court rulings and legal documents as precedents to arrive at this ruling; but in 1962, when the Supreme Court struck down voluntary prayer in schools, it did so without using any such precedent

Why may not the Bible, and especially the New Testament, without note or comment, be read and taught as a divine revelation in [schools] – its general precepts expounded, its evidences explained and its glorious principles of morality inculcated?...Where can the purest principles of morality be learned so clearly or so perfectly as from the New Testament?

Vidal v. Girard's Executors, 1844
Unanimous Decision Commending and Encouraging the Use of the
Bible in Government-Run Schools

Foreigners

The Americans combine the notions of Christianity and of liberty so intimately in their minds that it is impossible to make them conceive the one without the other.

Upon my arrival in the United States, the religious aspect of the country was the first thing that struck my attention; and the longer I stayed there, the more did I perceive the great political consequences resulting from this state of things, to which I was unaccustomed. In France I had almost always seen the spirit of religion and the spirit of freedom pursuing courses diametrically opposed to each other; but in America I found that they were intimately united, and that they reigned in common over the same country.

ALEXIS DE TOCQUEVILLE
French observer of America in 1831, author of Democracy in America

There is no country in which the people are so religious as in the United States...The great number of religious societies existing in the United States is truly surprising: there are some of them for everything; for instance, societies to distribute the Bible; to distribute tracts; to encourage religious journals; to convert, civilize, educate;...to take care of their widows and orphans; to preach, extend, purify, preserve, reform the faith; to build chapels, endow congregations, support seminaries;...to establish Sunday schools;...to prevent drunkenness, etc.

ACHILLE MURAT
French observer of America in 1832

BLESSED IS THE NATION WHOSE GOD IS THE LORD

PSALM 33:12A

IF MY PEOPLE WHO ARE CALLED BY MY NAME WILL HUMBLE THEMSELVES, AND PRAY AND SEEK MY FACE, AND TURN FROM THEIR WICKED WAYS, THEN I WILL HEAR FROM HEAVEN, AND WILL FORGIVE THEIR SIN AND HEAL THEIR LAND.

2 CHRONICLES 7:14

TO LEARN HOW TO BEGIN A RELATIONSHIP WITH CHRIST, CALL 1-888-NEED-HIM.
HOBBY LOBBY, HEMISPHERES AND MARDEL STORES · 7707 S.W. 44TH STREET · OKLAHOMA CITY, OK 73179
WWW.HOBBYLOBBY.COM/MINISTRYPROJECTS · IN ASSOCIATION WITH WWW.WALLBUILDERS.COM
FOR SOURCE REFERENCES, PLEASE REFER TO WWW.HOBBYLOBBY.COM/MINISTRYPROJECTS

1

FOUR HUNDRED NINETY COMPLIMENTS, FORTY-ONE COMPLAINTS

This is the story of Hobby Lobby's full-page newspaper advertisements at Easter, at Christmas, and on the Fourth of July. It's the story of how the ads created a fascinating debate in the minds of thinking people everywhere. Just the act of running a particular ad in papers across the country sparked a healthy outpouring of letters and e-mails to our Hobby Lobby home office in Oklahoma City. We received as many as a thousand letters whenever we ran one of these ads. I read each letter and kept the more notable ones, believing that someday they would make an interesting book. That's what you are holding.

The first ad was created in 1996 and appeared at Christmas and Easter in all the newspapers in which we advertised. Our first Fourth of July ad was created in 2006 with the help of the Wallbuilders ministry. What is interesting about that ad is that it created more than four times as many complaints as we had ever received in response to any of our other ads.

The ad was entitled "In God We Trust," and it included nineteen historical quotes. At the top we presented quotes from five of our early presidents.

"It is the duty of all nations to acknowledge the providence of Almighty God, to obey His will, to be grateful for His benefits, and humbly to implore His protection and favor."

GEORGE WASHINGTON, Commander in Chief in the American Revolution, Signer of the Constitution, First President of the United States

"We have no government armed with power capable of contending with human passions unbridled by morality and religion. Our Constitution was made only for a moral and religious people. It is wholly inadequate to the government of any other."

JOHN ADAMS, Signer of the Declaration of Independence, One of the two signers of the Bill of Rights, Second President of the United States

"And can the liberties of a nation be thought secure when we have removed their only firm basis, a conviction in the minds of the people that these liberties are of the gifts of God? That they are not to be violated but with His wrath? Indeed I tremble for my country when I reflect that God is just; that His justice cannot sleep forever."

THOMAS JEFFERSON, Signer and the principal author of the Declaration of Independence, Third President of the United States

"Before any man can be considered a member of civil society, he must be considered as a subject of the Governor of the Universe."

JAMES MADISON, Signer of the Constitution, Fourth President of the United States

"Is it not that in the chain of human events, the birthday of the nation is indissolubly linked with the birthday of the Savior?—that it forms a leading event in the progress of the Gospel dispensation? Is it not that the Declaration of Independence first organized the social compact on the foundation of the Redeemer's mission upon earth?—that it laid the cornerstone of human government upon the first precepts of Christianity?"

JOHN QUINCY ADAMS, Statesman, Diplomat, Sixth President of the United States

We followed these presidential quotes with quotes from a sampling of the Founding Fathers:

"An appeal to arms and to the God of hosts is all that is left us!... Sir, we are not weak if we make a proper use of those means which the God of nature hath placed in our power.... Besides sir, we shall not fight our battles alone. There is a just God who presides over the destinies of nations and who will raise up friends to fight our battles for us.... Is life so dear, or peace so sweet as to be purchased at the price of chains and slavery? Forbid it. Almighty God I know not what course others may take; but as for me, give me liberty or give me death!!!"

PATRICK HENRY, Patriot and Statesman

"To the kindly influence of Christianity we owe that degree of civil freedom, and political and social happiness which mankind now enjoys.... Whenever the pillars of Christianity shall be overthrown, our present republican forms of government—and all blessings which flow from them—must fall with them."

JEDEDIAH MORSE, Patriot and Educator, Called "The Father of American Geography"

"I lived, sir, a long time, and the longer I live, the more convincing proofs I see of this truth; that God governs the affairs of men. If a sparrow cannot fall to the ground without His notice, is it probable that an empire can rise without His aid? We've been assured in the sacred writings that unless the Lord builds the house, they labor in vain who build it. I firmly believe this, and I also believe that without His concurring aid we shall succeed in this political building no better than the builders of Babel."

BENJAMIN FRANKLIN, Signer of the Declaration of Independence and the Constitution

Right next to the quotes from these Founding Fathers, we included some quotes from Supreme Court justices:

"The Bible is the best of all books, for it is the word of God and teaches us the way to be happy in this world and in the next. Continue therefore to read it and to regulate your life by its precepts. Providence has given to our people the choice of their rulers, and it is the duty, as well as the privilege and interest of our Christian nation, to select and prefer Christians for their rulers."

JOHN JAY, Co-Author of the Federalist Papers, First Chief Justice of the U.S. Supreme Court

"Human law must rest its authority ultimately upon the authority of that law which is Divine.... Far from being rivals or enemies, religion and law are twin sisters, friends, and mutual assistants. Indeed these two sciences run into each other."

JAMES WILSON, Signer of the Declaration of Independence and the Constitution, Original Justice on the U.S. Supreme Court

"One of the beautiful boasts of our municipal jurisprudence is that Christianity is a part of the Common Law.... There never has been a period in which the Common Law did not recognize Christianity as lying at its foundations.... I verily believe Christianity necessary to the support of civil society."

JOSEPH STORY, U.S. Supreme Court Justice, Father of American Jurisprudence, Placed on the Court by President James Madison

On the lower half of our full-page ad, we went on to feature two quotes from Congress:

"We are a Christian people...not because the law demands it, not to gain exclusive benefits, or to avoid legal disabilities, but from choice and education; and in a land thus universally Christian, what is to be expected, what desired, but that we shall pay due regard to Christianity."

Senate Judiciary Committee Report, January 19, 1853

"At the time of the adoption of the Constitution and the amendments, the universal sentiment was that Christianity should be encouraged.... In this age there can be no substitute for Christianity.... That was the religion of the founders of the republic and they expected it to remain the religion of their descendants."

House Judiciary Committee Report, March 27, 1854

Then we added two quotes from the world of education:

"Let every student be plainly instructed and earnestly pressed to consider well the main end of his life and studies is to know God and Jesus Christ which is eternal life (John 17:3) and therefore to lay Christ in the bottom as the only foundation of all sound knowledge and learning. And seeing the Lord only giveth wisdom, let everyone seriously set himself by prayer in secret to seek it of Him (Proverbs 2, 3). Everyone shall so exercise himself in reading the Scriptures twice a day that he shall be ready to give such an account of his proficiency therein."

Harvard, 1636 Student Guidelines

"All the scholars are required to live a religious and blameless life according to the rules of God's Word, diligently reading the Holy Scriptures, that fountain of Divine light and truth, and constantly attending all the duties of religion."

Yale, 1787 Student Guidelines

We also included information from two Supreme Court rulings:

"There is no dissonance in these [legal] declarations.... These are not individual sayings, declarations of private persons; they are organic [legal, governmental] utterances; they speak the voice of the entire people.... These, and many other matters which might be noticed, add a volume of unofficial declarations to the mass of organic utterances that this is a Christian nation."

CHURCH OF THE HOLY TRINITY V. U.S., 1892, unanimous decision declaring America a Christian nation. Significantly, the U.S. Supreme Court cited dozens of court rulings and legal documents as precedents to arrive at this ruling; but in 1962 when the Supreme Court struck down voluntary prayer in schools, it did so without using any such precedent.

"Why may not the Bible, and especially the New Testament, without note or comment, be read and taught as a divine revelation in [schools]—its general precepts expounded, its evidences explained, and its glorious principles of morality inculcated?...Where can the purest principles of morality be learned so clearly or so perfectly as from the New Testament?"

VIDAL V. GIRARD'S EXECUTORS, 1844, unanimous decision commending and encouraging the use of the Bible in Government run schools

Our final quotes were placed under the heading "Foreigners."

"The Americans combine the notions of Christianity and of liberty so intimately in their minds that it is impossible to make them conceive the one without the other.

"Upon my arrival in the United States, the religious aspect of the country was the first thing that struck my attention; and the longer I stayed there, the more did I perceive the great political consequences resulting from this state of things, to which I was unaccustomed. In France I had almost always seen the spirit of religion and the spirit of freedom pursuing courses diametrically opposed to each other; but in America I found that they were intimately united, and that they reigned in common over the same country."

ALEXIS DE TOCQUEVILLE, French observer of America in 1831, author of
Democracy in America

"There is no country in which the people are so religious as in the United States.... The great number of religious societies existing in the United States is truly surprising; there are some of them for everything; for instance, societies to distribute the Bible, to distribute tracts, to encourage religious journals, to convert, civilize, educate;...to take care of their widows and orphans; to preach, extend, purify, preserve, reform the faith; to build chapels, endow congregations, support seminaries;...to establish Sunday schools;...to prevent drunkenness, etc."

ACHILLE MURAT, French observer of America in 1832

At the very bottom of the full-page ad, we concluded with the following words:

Blessed is the nation whose God is the Lord
PSALM 33:12A

If My people, who are called by My name will humble themselves, and pray, and seek My face, and turn from their wicked ways, then I will hear from Heaven, and will forgive their sins and heal their land.
2 CHRONICLES 7:14

To learn how to begin a relationship with Christ, call 1-888-NEED HIM

Hobby Lobby, Hemispheres and Mardel Stores—7707 SW 44th Street, Oklahoma City OK 73179
www.hobbylobby.com/ministryprojects—in association with www.wallbuilders.com
For source references, please refer to www.hobbylobby.com/ministryprojects

Because the number of complaints this ad generated was so much more than our other ads, I couldn't help but be transfixed by the content of those complaints. So I decided I needed to step up to the plate and help explain what is behind the words that we wrote and why we did it.

As I read the letters of criticism over and over, a pattern began to unfold in my mind. The letters of complaint seemed to fall into three general categories:

1. Those who thought we were being divisive and argued that we should seek to "coexist" with one another.
2. Those who felt the issue was one of separation of church and state. That a business shouldn't have a "religion" anymore than a school or a government.
3. Those who argued from an atheistic viewpoint and didn't like what our ad had to say.

Here are a few of the letters we received from the first category. I have edited them for content and brevity, and, of course, I will not reveal any names. I have also highlighted the points we want to address later in the book with bold italics.

Dear Sirs:

How can this be a Christian nation if not everyone is a Christian? Why don't you just advertise your store and not religion? I guess you were trying to make a difference, but **you left a lot of people out.** You need to make some friends that are not Christian. **Explore all religions. They all come down to: "We are all connected."** Don't worry, everything is as it should be. Maybe apologize to those who have been offended.

· · ·

Dear Hobby Lobby:

I was floored to see Hobby Lobby's full-page ad in the *New York Times* yesterday. While I appreciate you supporting this great newspaper with your advertising dollars, the substance of your ad was **divisive** in America. In good conscience and as a Christian mother of three young children who will make their way in this country well after you and I are long gone, I can no longer shop in your store and support this agenda, of which I was unaware. You must realize that all your profit-making is due to the **multicultural and open nature of American society. Why promote this divisiveness?** I scrapbook (and shop in your store) with a group of twelve women here in Franklin from all walks of life. **This ad will trouble the Jewish girls who shop with us, the Catholic girls, the Mideastern girls whose husbands are professionals at Vanderbilt and who already feel out of place as Muslims in Williamson County.** I am really so puzzled and disappointed to learn this is the agenda of a company I really value.

· · ·

Dear Hobby Lobby:

I saw your ad in *USA Today* and quite frankly, you will never see me in your stores again. If you were truly Christians you would have used your money to help some of the millions of starving people in the world instead of using it proselytizing in order to drum up business. **If Jesus** *were around today undoubtedly he would preach respecting all religions that taught people to be good and caring.* Your ad is a slap in the face to all of us "non-believers."

. . .

To Whom It May Concern:

I wish to express my concern with regards to the aforementioned ad. As a Christian, I resent for my fellow non-Christian Americans (and I am sure non-Christian Hobby Lobby shoppers) the ad's implications that the United States is a Christian country. *Our forefathers founded this country for religious freedom, I believe, as many Christians do, that means any religion—not just Christian. I listen to the Christian music played in Hobby Lobby and am not particularly offended but do wonder what non-Christian shoppers think of it.* I just need to express my concern and feel just expressing it to the store manager is not enough, since I am sure he does not have any real input on policy.

I see that these writers and those like them generally have a *positive* view of religions. The argument they have is when one religion is favored over another, that gives them discomfort. I believe this group believes that the world would be a better place if religions would just get along with one another. There is a bumper sticker I am seeing more frequently that sums up this idea. It consists of only one word—*coexist*—and incorporates different religious symbols in the font for each letter. The idea is for us to all get along.

The letter writers in the second category in which we were critiqued argued for separation of church and state. This group takes a more *neutral* position on religion. Even though we are neither a church nor part of the state, the belief is that we as a business should not have a religious position. This group argues that just as schools and governments shouldn't advocate a religion, businesses also should be neutral when it comes to religion. Here are some of their letters:

Dear Hobby Lobby:

Your full-page ad in the July 3rd *USA Today* proposes that America is, or should be, a Christian based nation. By its date of issue [just prior to Independence Day] it also suggests those of other religious beliefs, or without religious convictions are something less than patriots. Shame on your corporate brain trust for allowing such nonsense to be published, even if they believe it. Our nation's laws are based on the Constitution. There are no statements within it that propose or support your contention. There is no mention of God in this foundational law document, and in fact the First Amendment is clearly opposed to a nation-based religion. "Congress shall make no law respecting the establishment of religion or prohibiting free exercise thereof..."

For every forefather's quote chosen in this ad, I can counter with another from the same person clearly indicating their insistence of *a separation of the church from the state*. For instance, John Adams: "Nothing is more dreaded than the national government meddling with religion." Also the 1797 **Treaty of Tripoli** that he signed and was unanimously approved by the U.S. Senate clearly stating the United States is not a Christian nation.

Because of your dishonest and divisive business practice I will not support your business any further. I will make your inappropriate and unpatriotic ad known to my students and colleagues. They can decide for themselves what the real costs of doing business with their coinage as well. You'll note that "In God We Trust" didn't exist then, only "E Pluribus Unum." A more unifying phrase, don't you think?

· · ·

Hi Folks:

I just wanted to respond to your full-page newspaper ad appearing so very ironically on the Fourth of July **suggesting that we essentially scrap our democracy for a theocracy**. I suggest you spend some time in Iran or Syria where they have functioning theocracies and see if you still think that is a good model for government. Of course you have a right to your view and to voice that belief. And I have a right to never shop in a Hobby Lobby again and to take out an ACLU membership in your name.

. . .

Dear Hobby Lobby:

When I was browsing the paper on July 4th I found an ad *against the division between church and state.* Being used to propaganda of this nature, I looked to see what Christian group had run the ad. Imagine my surprise to find it was a retail chain. The quotes in the article are the exact reason why there should be separation. Twisting statements made by our forefathers to appear we are only a Christian nation. They must have been aware this would happen and *made separation of church and state very clear* in our founding documents. *If we want to be a nation run by religion we might as well be Iran.* You can see how well that is working out for them. You have made your opinion clear. I am making mine. I will no longer shop at any of your stores. I will also tell everyone I know and ask that they tell ten people. I know you knew the backlash that would occur, so my e-mail won't really matter. But I was far too appalled not to reply to this insanity. Please *keep your Christian ideas in your church, and out of my government and my schools. I would rather we have and teach acceptance and tolerance instead.*

. . .

Dear Hobby Lobby:

Not everyone who has a hobby is interested in Christianity. *A business should keep its religion to itself—in fact a business should not HAVE a religion.* Do you require that all your employees follow your religion? If so, you are probably in violation of First Amendment rights. If we want religion, we will go to a religious organization. If we want hobby supplies—then we non-Christians will not go to Hobby Lobby.

The third and final category of letters were from those with an atheistic perspective. This group was definitely against any religion. Their view is that all religion is *bad,* therefore they obviously took offence at our ad. Here is a sampling:

• • •

Dear Hobby Lobby:

From your July 4th "message" it would appear that Hobby Lobby has embraced the dominionist movement and would like to see the ideas of fundamentalist extremists become a part of our government and law. If I am mistaken, by all means feel free to correct me. As an armchair Constitutional scholar and as a concerned citizen, *I see this movement as extremely damaging to our great nation. Its influence has had demonstrably negative effects on the rights of our citizens, and with our standing in the world community. Nations led by fundamentalist extremists, no matter what faith they embrace, have always been the source of profound human suffering. Always.* Had I known the advancement of such an agenda was a central company principle of Hobby Lobby, I would never have become a customer. You may be assured I will never patronize your business again.

• • •

Dear Hobby Lobby:

I didn't realize I would be supporting a Christian ministry by purchasing things from your store. From now on, I will get my hobby supplies [elsewhere]. I certainly would not want my money to be used to support superstition of any kind at a time when religions of all kinds are bringing civilization perilously close to the brink of destruction. Nor would I wish to contribute to the mental and moral abuse of children by preventing the development of their reality-testing skills or their ability to develop an ethical sense superior to the taboo morality of any religions.

All Bibles are human inventions and are among the most fallible and faulty products of human literature.... As you know, all children are born atheists and it is only by means of brainwashing such as you are funding and carrying out that they are seduced into the service of religious entrepreneurs. Children should be taught to use their powers of reason, not to abandon them. It is imperative that everyone abandon "faith" in favor of learning, evidence, and knowledge. It is imperative that the Bibles of mankind be studied scientifically. The greatest Bible scholars today are atheists—they know TOO much about Bibles!

It is too late in history to chase an illusion and think that we have an invisible friend hiding in the clouds. You are contributing to the collapse of civilization by promoting the scientific understanding of the twentieth century. Christianity and its failure of reality-testing brought about the fall of the Roman Empire. It may bring the fall of world civilization as well.

In sum, all of the sciences from archaeology to zoology show that Christianity is fundamentally untrue. All of modern philosophy and ethics show it is unjust and dangerous as well. I shall continue to warn my friends of the danger involved in doing business with Hobby Lobby.

As a member of the business world, I will from time to time read the latest business books or study business trends in order to keep up with the latest ideas. One of the ideas that has been around for a while is to focus on your existing customers as much or more than gaining new ones. It's said that it costs five times more to gain a new customer than to keep an existing one! Frequent flyer programs are an example of this kind of effort. The idea is to work hard to keep the customers you have. This begs the question, why in the world would we have an ad program that generated such complaints? That is what I want to address in this book.

Before we actually begin to answer the many questions that were raised, let's step back for a bit and let you in on how the holiday full-page ad came into existence at our Hobby Lobby headquarters. •

Discover the TRUE meaning of Christmas.

She will give birth to a son, and you are to give him the name Jesus,
because he will save his people from their sins.

Matthew 1:21

2

THE BIRTH OF AN AD

Those who regularly shop our Hobby Lobby stores know that we advertise routinely in local newspapers as well as online and through an extensive e-mail mailing list. People know to check out these ads to find out what's on sale and note other items of interest. But, of course, we also run ads at Christmas and Easter and on the Fourth of July that don't include sale items or special pricing. We just want to let people know that we love our Lord and we love our country. We're not saying every company should do it, but it felt like the right thing for us to do.

So how did an ad for a holiday come into existence? My father, David Green, held the answer to that question, so I invited him into the conference room at Hobby Lobby headquarters in Oklahoma City to take a stroll down memory lane with me. Knowing in advance the topics we would be discussing, we also invited my mother, Barbara, to join us as well.

HOW IT ALL BEGAN

• • •

"Tell me, Dad," I said once the three of us were settled into our seats, "what's your recollection of how we first got the ads started in the newspapers?"

I have always admired my dad as a man of action. He is also a man of few words. So I watched with interest as he thought back to our ad's beginning. After a bit of a pause, he said, "It was Christmas Day, 1995." He looked toward the ceiling for a clear memory of the occasion. "I was sitting at the kitchen table, reading through the Christmas Day newspaper during a quiet moment in the morning. The *Daily Oklahoman* is one of the most conservative newspapers in the nation, so what I saw surprised me. I thumbed through the pages, and I was bombarded by all the advertisements featuring reindeer, snowmen, Christmas trees, and, of course, Santa Claus. There wasn't even a 'Merry Christmas' to be found in the entire paper. 'Seasons Greetings? Yes. But no 'Merry Christmas.'

"That's when it struck me. I wasn't proclaiming Him either.

"Here we were selling all sorts of crafts that related to all these different ways to celebrate Christmas, and God needed to get my attention through the lack of any testimony in the newspaper. When I look back on that whole experience I remember that at that moment I felt *commissioned* by God to do something very intentionally the next Christmas."

"That's a good word to describe how serious you felt about creating an ad that would let people know where you stood regarding the Lord," my mom commented on Dad's emphasis of the word *commissioned*.

I agreed. "I know you've written about this in your own book, Dad. This is how you described it:

It didn't seem right. Wasn't the arrival of the Baby in Bethlehem the whole origin of Christmas? Then why were they taking up page after page talking about everything from politics to stock-market prospects in the year to come?

Well, I couldn't do anything about the news columns or the editorial page, but I was, after all, an advertiser in this newspaper, as well as more than 250 other papers across the country. Every week I was already paying money to put out my message about the coming week's sale items. Couldn't I spend more of my money to spotlight the eternal importance of Christmas?

I knew, of course, that some people would say a "secular business" should not get involved in such a thing. But I've never been real fond of the word secular. I looked it up in one dictionary that defined it as, among other meanings, "without God." Was that what I wanted Hobby Lobby to be? Not at all.

I began to talk with [my wife] Barbara and the children about an advertising approach. "I think we need to do something that's more important than commerce," I said. "Nobody else is talking about the real meaning of the holidays that are so significant to us as merchants. We bring in a lot of money thanks to Christmas and Easter. Let's be bold about what the days truly mean."

They agreed with me, so we prepared a modest ad—only about six inches square.[1]

"It was a quarter page ad in the *Daily Oklahoman*. It simply stated:

As you celebrate this Christmas season in the warmth of family and home, may you be drawn to the Savior; He who left the beauty of Heaven on our behalf and became like us, that we might become like Him. If you know Jesus as your Savior, then this season already has a special meaning. If you do not, we encourage you find a Bible-believing church in your community, and to discover a relationship this Christmas with the God who loves you more than you can begin to imagine.

Hobby Lobby Stores, Inc.
7707 SW 44th Street
Oklahoma City, Oklahoma 73162
www.hobbylobby.com

"I knew we had to do it," Dad reemphasized. "And we've been doing it ever since. I've been especially excited about the look of the ads over the last few years as Darsee [my sister] has taken over the leadership of the Art Department.

"We do it because we believe it's the right thing to do," Dad continued. "If it's right, we do it without regard to the consequences."

BEGINNING THE FOURTH OF JULY AD
. . .

"What do you remember about the beginnings of the Fourth of July ad?" I asked.

"What I remember is feeling concerned about where our country was going," Dad replied, shaking his head. "Listening to the news on the radio or reading it in the newspapers was discouraging. I remember getting really upset when I heard about how people were trying to change our history books so they wouldn't include the faith of our Founding Fathers," Dad said.

Mom interjected, "We saw a film at church right around that time that really opened our eyes to what was going on in our nation."

"Yes. It was a film featuring David Barton of the Wallbuilders ministry, and it was centered on all these people of faith who were signers of our U.S. Constitution. It really got my attention, and I decided we needed to make a statement about the godly heritage of our wonderful country."

Dad stopped for a moment, took a sip of water, and leaned over in my direction. "Do you remember what happened next, Steve?"

"Yes, I do," I smiled as I replied. "You assigned me to get in touch with David Barton, which I did. After an extended phone conversation, we invited him to come here to Oklahoma City so we could put our heads together in order to create a Fourth of July ad that would express how we feel about our country."

Dad nodded in agreement. "Yes, that's the way I remember it as well. As I recall, he brought a lot of material with him—letters, quotes, all sorts of testimonies from all kinds of famous Americans. The more we discussed it, the more we liked the idea of quotes about our Christian nation from the people who were in leadership—presidents, judges, congressmen, and the like.

"We ran our first Fourth of July ad in 2006 in the Dallas and Oklahoma City newspapers. The next year we went all out and ran it in *USA Today*. The following year we chose the *New York Times* and the *Los Angeles Times*. After that, it ran in all the papers in which we advertise. And, by the way, we always advertise in the leading newspaper in a particular city, no matter the extra expense."

THE ADS HAVE IMPACT IN MANY WAYS
• • •

"Back to the early days of the first holiday ads—those led to taking a stand in other ways, didn't it, Dad?" I prompted.

"That's correct. It wasn't long after the ads started running that the Lord convicted me about our stores being open on Sundays. I started running the figures and realized that if we closed on Sundays, we'd be walking away from about one hundred million dollars a year. But do you know what, Steve? From the time I was a little boy, I knew this one thing to be true—God blesses doing right!"

"So you're saying it's worth it—even from a financial perspective," I summarized.

"That's right. Plus, when you figure that these days, it costs us about one and a half million dollars to run each ad, we're making a serious financial commitment. But we believe it's the right thing to do. And I firmly believe it is one of the reasons God has blessed our business."

I remember those days. By 1998 we had a more public profile as a company, and Dad was beginning to feel convicted about taking our employees away from their church and their families on Sunday. Gradually we began closing our stores on Sunday until it was a full company-wide practice.

We did it because we wanted to. Because we felt it was the right thing to do. No one forced us, and our employees truly appreciated it. God has provided for our business in a wonderful way, so even though we miss out on that Sunday revenue, the Lord takes care of us!

Another direct result of the ad campaign was the impact it had on my older brother, Mart. When he saw how people were scrambling to get additional copies of the ads we were producing, he realized how important it was to have all sorts of media available for folks to use who want to make their beliefs known. Mart's idea went a lot further than newspaper advertising. He began exploring the world of television by making commercials for businesses to use in order to make a statement of their belief. It was at that point he was inspired even further—how about a *movie*?

Mart established his own movie production company and produced a movie called *End of the Spear.* It's the story of five Christian missionaries who visited the Waodani Indians in South America—at the time, during the 1950s, the most violent people on earth. Sadly, all five of the missionaries were killed while trying to share the Gospel with these savages. But the beauty of this story is that subsequently the message of the good news did pierce their hearts, and they embraced the Lord Jesus as their Savior. The movie chronicles that story as well as the remarkable transformation that resulted.

"We mustn't forget how the ad impacted other ministries as well," Mom interjected. "Think about how the ad created a bridge between us and the folks over at the ministry, *Every Home for Christ.*"

Dad paused a moment, seeming to take it all in. "You are so right," he nodded sweetly toward my mom. "I'll never forget when we received that letter from Dick Eastman, their president. It meant so much to me, we framed it and it hangs on our wall here at our offices."

The letter Dad is referring to said the following:

January 6, 1998

Dear Mr. Green:

I want to commend you and your company for the unusually simple, yet powerfully profound introduction to Jesus in your one-page advertisement that I happened to see Christmas Day in the *Denver Post.* This succinct message was perhaps the finest Christmas communication introducing the reality of Christ that I can recall seeing. My prayer is

A SLATE WIPED CLEAN

✝ ✝ ✝

REPENT, THEN, AND TURN TO GOD, SO THAT YOUR SINS MAY BE WIPED OUT,
THAT TIMES OF REFRESHING MAY COME FROM THE LORD.
ACTS 3:19

that it will continue to impact the minds of those who saw the message and draw them to a personal encounter with Jesus Christ.

Your message especially blessed me because Every Home for Christ (a fifty-year-old ministry formerly known as World Literature Crusade) seeks to place a simple printed message of who Jesus is and how to receive Him as Savior in every home on earth. Thus far, that has happened in an estimated 900 million households in more than 180 countries where two printed Gospel booklets have been given per home (one for adults and one for children).

Because each message (in the indigenous language spoken by the people of a particular region) includes a decision card with the address of the nearest Every Home Crusade office, we receive hundreds of thousands of decision cards per year. (Last year the total was actually 1.4 million, or over 4,000 each day). Each decision card is followed up with a four-part Bible correspondence course that provides initial discipleship information to help those who respond become maturing followers of Jesus Christ.

I realize you're a very busy man, but I've enclosed a copy of my latest book, *Beyond Imagination: A Simple Plan to Save the World,* that I thought might be of encouragement to you. It documents quite a number of moving accounts of what has happened and is happening globally as the printed message introducing Jesus Christ is taken home by home until entire nations, one village and town at a time, are saturated with the good news.

Again, I commend you on the excellent Christmas message communicated in the advertisement on Christmas Day.

May God bless you richly in your business as you seek to honor Christ.

Sincerely in Christ,

Dick Eastman
President
Every Home for Christ

"I read his book," Dad continued, "and I was really moved by the way the ministry operates. We prayed about it, and we decided to get involved with them as financial supporters. We have seen the message of the Gospel penetrate millions of homes. The ministry has done studies on its distributions, and the findings have shown that three to four people are exposed to the literature for every home that is reached—and they are pouring literature into millions of homes all over the world!"

"So it can't be overlooked that our strategic partnership with Every Home for Christ is a direct result of the one-page ad at Christmas," I summarized.

"That's exactly right," Mom and Dad replied heartily in unison.

And, of course, one cannot overlook the mountain of mail we have received over the years filled with positive affirmation concerning the ads themselves. Everything from people who were momentarily touched by the spirit of our ads, to folks who speak of a major change in their lives as a result. Be sure to see the last chapter of this book, where we will include some of our favorite letters.

Yes, a great deal has resulted from a thought in my father's mind while reading the newspaper on Christmas Day.

Let me tell you about our most popular ad of all time. •

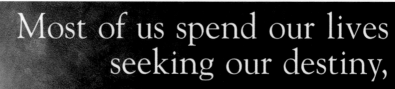

Most of us spend our lives
seeking our destiny,

One Man created His own.

It began in
a manger
and led to
a cross,
and it
included
you.

You too have a destiny
and someday . . . someday soon,
your destiny will cross with His.

3

THE MOST POPULAR AD

Christmas of 1998 would be the occasion for the most popular ad Hobby Lobby has ever run. To this day, there is something so captivating, so engaging, so engrossing about this sentiment that we receive requests for copies of it regularly.

Here is the copy:

> Most of us spend our lives seeking our destiny.
> One Man created His own.
> It began in a manger and led to a cross, and it included you.
> You, too, have a destiny and someday...someday soon,
> Your destiny will cross with His.

The copy sits to the right of a beautiful piece of artwork. It depicts the Lord Jesus as a child, maybe two years old, in Joseph's workshop. Joseph, in a robe of deep orange with a pale blue sash, is hard at work, doing carpentry while standing at a worktable. Little Jesus, in a light yellow robe with a blue sash, crouches next to

Joseph, playing on the floor with three large spike-sized nails. A bright light is shining through the window from the left, creating a shadow behind little Jesus. But instead of the shadow being in the shape of a human, it is in the shape of a cross.

One of the key players in the creation of this ad, as well as so many of our early ads, was Bill Hane. He served as our advertising manager at Hobby Lobby for many years and accomplished an exemplary job during his tenure with us. Bill is now working in a different world than hobbies; he is a part of the oil business. But recently I had a chance to sit down with him over lunch and stroll down memory lane regarding the full-page ads.

Once seated at a booth in the restaurant, Bill and I shared pleasantries and then ordered our meals. The waiter brought our beverages, so Bill drank his iced tea while I sipped my lemonade. I gave him a moment and then began a flurry of questions.

"What's your earliest recollection of the ads, Bill?" I asked.

"Well, we had that small paragraph in the Christmas 1996 local paper," he replied. "David [my dad] was pleased with the way that was received, so we created an ad for Easter of 1997. That, too, was well received, so David asked me to present him an idea that we could use for our Christmas 1997 ad. I came up with the copy that said:

> When man reaches for God, we call it religion.
> When God reaches for man, we call it Christmas.

"David liked the idea," Bill continued. "'Let's do something a little more artistic,' was his suggestion. I gave the assignment to one of our artists, Thereon James, who came up with the hands reaching for the baby Jesus. The art was also very well received, so David decided to expand the half-page ad to a full-page one. Christmas of '97 was our first full-page ad, and we haven't looked back since!"

His eyes lit up with genuine affection and enthusiasm as he spoke of these projects. I was clearly tapping into the man's passion. These ads were a labor of love for Bill.

"What was next up on our ad calendar?" I encouraged him to continue.

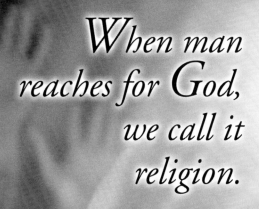

When man reaches for God, we call it religion.

When God reaches for man, we call it Christmas

Through an act of love, greater than our minds can comprehend, you have been called by the great heart of God.

He knew you before you were born; He called you to Himself through His Son, Jesus Christ;

and He calls you today, at this season of celebration, to know Jesus as Savior and Lord.

You have been called: How will you respond?

If you would like to know Jesus as Savior and Lord, call the *Need Him Ministry* at **1-888-NEED HIM**

"Easter of 1998—that was a very special ad for me personally," Bill answered.

"Tell me about it," I urged.

"It was all centered on an angel emptying the tomb. We came up with the copy that said:

No one empties a tomb like Jesus

"And at the bottom of the ad, we added the words:

He lives! Does He live within your heart?

"Why was this ad so personal to you?" I asked him once he finished his description of the ad.

"That year I had experienced a difficult personal loss," he replied quietly. "I lost my best friend. He died in a plane crash in a cornfield in Nebraska. His wife and his daughter survived, but the whole story was so painful."

We sat quietly for a minute, and then Bill continued. "It was at the same time we were designing this ad. I wanted the power of resurrection to come across in a strong way. So I went to our artist, Thereon, again. This time my instructions were clear: Draw me the biggest angel you can!"

And that's exactly what he did. "The muscles in the angel's arms are bulging with strength," Bill continued. "It brought encouragement to many of our customers—but special encouragement to me."

"Which brings us to Christmas of 1998," I said, perfectly timed as the waiter brought us our sandwiches.

"Our most popular ad of all time," Bill nodded knowingly.

"Tell me about how the ad was conceived," I asked.

"I saw it in my head," he said, looking off into the distance. "I saw a common carpenter with a common child—yet it was such an uncommon destiny."

"I shared the concept with Thereon. 'I see a carpenter at work in his shop while his son is at his side playing with nails.' Thereon was scribbling notes vigorously as I shared my vision with him.

No One
Empties A Tomb
Like Jesus

"For if you confess with your mouth
that Jesus is Lord and believe
in your heart that God
raised him from the dead,
you will be saved."

Romans 10:9

He
Lives!
Does He live
within your heart?

"The carpenter and the child are by a window that lets in a marvelous ray of light," I added.

"Over the next few days, Thereon started submitting sketches from his sketchbook, showing me how he could take my thoughts and transfer them into art. He probably sketched eight or ten of them for us to look at."

I interrupted with a question at this point. "Bill, where did the inspiration come from for the actual figures he drew as Joseph and Jesus?"

"That's an interesting question," Bill responded, "because both of the characters were based on real people. Thereon and I kept going round and round about how old Joseph would have been when Jesus was a young child. In the earliest sketches, he looked too old to me, so I told Thereon we needed a younger man who could be our model. He agreed.

"That's when it hit me. I have a friend whom I've known since I was a child who is an actual carpenter. Plus, he has a ministry where he dresses up in the robes of the Bible times and teaches groups from the Gospel of Matthew. I made a phone call, and the next thing you know, Thereon and I were able to take photographs of him in his biblical costume, which provided the model for Joseph."

"So how about Jesus as a little boy?" I asked. "Can you remember how that came into being?"

A big smile appeared on Bill's face. I could just tell this part of the story would be particularly fascinating.

"The inspiration for the little boy was *my* little boy," Bill said with a look any proud father could identify. "We took photographs of my son Andrew so Thereon would once again have a model from which he could work."

"That must have been exciting to see your son in the poster," I mused.

"Yes. But you don't know the full story, Steve. My wife had some very serious health issues for several years in our marriage. Both of us had prayed for quite some time that God would give us another child. After we had been married for around ten years, in August 1997, to be exact, a baby arrived to us as a foster child. His mother had recently passed away, and his father was an alcoholic."

"So how did Andrew go from being a foster child to being your adopted son?" I questioned out loud.

"Weeks and months went by with little Andrew in our home. We were so blessed to have this special guy in our family. Meanwhile, his father was still battling his alcoholism. One day the dad contacted us to tell us that if we'd be interested, he would be willing to give us all adoptive rights to Andrew. I'm sure it was a difficult decision for the dad to make, but it was an easy one for us to answer. We would gladly adopt Andrew as our own son."

"Wow," I said softly.

"I should also tell you that Andrew's biological father passed away only three years later. My wife and I both felt that this entire circumstance was the hand of God at work. The expression we like to use is: God's timeline is always right."

"And that's how your son became the model for the young Jesus on our Christmas ad," I concluded for him. I thought it was a beautiful account and was ready to press on to other items to discuss.

"No, we're not finished yet," Bill confessed.

"Okay—go on," I encouraged.

"I took a bunch of photographs of our son Andrew playing on the floor with long nails—just like it would appear in the ad. But as Thereon and I looked at the photos, we both thought we might need to see another option of what this young Jesus could look like. We liked the age of Andrew, and we got some really good poses that Thereon could work with. It was Andrew's face and straight hair that made us wonder if there was another way.

"That's when Thereon came up with an idea of his own. He went home and did some photographing of another subject. He brought them back to me, and we discovered the inspiration for the face of young Jesus: it was Thereon's little daughter!

"That charming, angelic face of Jesus in that ad belongs to his sweet little Amber," Bill continued. "She was the right age. The photos turned out perfectly for what we were looking for, so we put Amber's face, head, and hair on Andrew's body. The result was the exact look we had been going for."

"No one ever commented on the face of little Jesus looking like the face of a little girl?" I asked with a smile.

"None," Bill replied emphatically. "But we did get some folks who wrote in to register their surprise that little Jesus was a *blond*!"

At that point we both had a hearty laugh. We both knew there was no "in-between the lines" hidden message in young Jesus being blond.

"One last point about the artwork itself," Bill added, "was the addition of the sun casting a shadow on little Jesus that we shaped, not like his body, but like a cross. Steve, that idea came from your brother Mart. As soon as he offered it, Thereon made a sketch of it, and we all loved it.

"Well, we ran the ad that we entitled 'Destiny' as a full page in the newspapers for Christmas of 1998. And as you have already noted, Steve, the response was huge. To this day it remains our most popular ad of all time."

"We got a bunch of mail, didn't we?" I asked.

"Yes, and it was overwhelmingly positive. But we did get some mail from folks who didn't like us taking such a forthright stand for Christianity and the true meaning of Christmas," he answered.

One of the things I had come to appreciate about Bill was the thoughtful way he would respond to the critiques. So I asked Bill about it.

"Trying to respond to those people became a real journey for me. I was raised in a strict Christian home, grew up and became a schoolteacher for nine years. Then I came to work at Hobby Lobby, and the next thing you know, I was answering letters containing people's objections to what we were doing! I wasn't fully prepared for what I called the 'in your face' type of opposition, so I sure learned a lot while I was doing it."

"Give me some ideas of the kinds of things you learned while answering these folks," I inquired.

"Well, first of all, I learned that you don't need to win every argument. You make a mistake if you assume they want your opinion! Second, I learned that you are not at war. My goal was to give an accurate and Christlike response to these folks. I wanted to open up a dialog and start an ongoing discussion. To me, that is the exact opposite of a letter that is filled with put-downs.

"More and more I began to argue from the position of public discourse. Is it permissible for the owner of a private company to express themselves in the public arena? The answer is unquestionably yes.

"Of course, there are people who don't want answers. They just want to argue and issue their put-downs. It forced me to ask the question, from what lens do we see things? Rather than looking through the lens of harshness, defensiveness, and criticism, I simply attempted to speak the truth in love."

I interjected, "What did we do for folks who genuinely wanted to know more about the Christian faith?"

"At the bottom of every ad we did, we placed a way for folks to get some help. We were made aware of a group called 1-800-NEED HIM that specialized in following up on people with spiritual questions. They manned the phones twenty-four hours a day, seven days a week with godly, mature counselors who could answer questions as well as lead people to begin a relationship with the Lord Jesus. It was the perfect match—our ads and their 800 number."

"So 'Destiny' really has been a popular ad, hasn't it?" I said as I began to wind down our lunchtime meeting.

"It really was a winner. Steve, as you well know, the ad has been reproduced all over the world. It's been made into posters. It's been made into framed art. It's even been made into a stamp. Hobby Lobby is regularly asked if the ad can be reproduced for churches, schools, businesses, and all manner of uses. And to the best of my knowledge, we always tried to be accommodating.

"It's humbling for me to see how the ad still has a deep impact on people's lives. About a year ago, I visited a friend in Edmond, Oklahoma. As we talked about a variety of subjects, out of the blue, he suddenly said to me, 'My wife and I went through a tough time not too long ago. That picture helped us get through it.' Of course, he was talking about 'Destiny,' though he didn't know I had a part to play in it."

If I wasn't mistaken, it looked like my friend Bill Hane got a little choked up at that point. As I watched him look back over such an amazing part of his vocational life, I could tell that he was deeply impacted by the power of the one-page ads that he had been a part of over the years.

Yes, there are many wonderful, heartwarming, even life-changing stories as a result of Hobby Lobby's commitment to boldly share their faith during the holiday seasons. But it is time to turn our attention to those who wrote us expressing criticism about what we said. Using our Fourth of July ad as their point of contention, let's unwrap some answers to their all-important questions. •

FOR GOD SO LOVED THE WORLD HE GAVE

acceptance
peace
mercy
confidence
purpose
forgiveness
simplicity
hope
relief
comfort
equality
life

HIS SON.

This Easter, we encourage you to believe in the love that sent Jesus Christ.
Accept the hope. Accept the joy. Accept the LIFE!

4

ALL RELIGIONS ARE GOOD

Our letters of complaint were varied in content, but it became apparent as we read each one that most seemed to fall into one of three categories: (1) religions are good, so let's just coexist, (2) keep church and state separate, which is a more neutral view of religion, and (3) religions are bad, the view of atheists.

I've set aside a full chapter to explore each of these three complaints, but before we get into the first argument, it would be wise to take a few moments to lay down a foundation for what it is we want to explore. Specifically, let's talk about the term *worldview*.

WHAT DO WE MEAN BY WORLDVIEW?
· · ·

What is meant when we use the word *worldview*? In my reading, I found the definition and explanation of Christian Overman and Don Johnson to be very helpful:

Somewhere deep inside our minds, we all have a frame of reference that affects the way we look at everything. This is as true for the Christian as for everyone else. Whether we are conscious of it or not, this mental frame of reference provides latitude and longitude lines from which we get our bearings as we navigate throughout our inner world of thought. The subconscious mind never fails to consult this internal navigation system when issues of importance confront us. It is a mental grid which allows us to make sense of our surroundings, our relationships, our jobs, our dreams and decisions. This inner frame of reference—this conceptual window through which we perceive and interpret all of reality—is a **worldview**.[2]

Overman and Christian go on to explain worldviews with these thoughts:

At its core, worldviews are made up of conscious beliefs or unconscious assumptions that are held by faith.... When it comes to mental perceptions about reality, there is no such thing as an absolute "unbeliever." We are all believers in something. Even if that something happens to be "nothing"!...

Based on this concept of worldviews and our particular approach to biblical worldview integration, our working definition for the term "worldview" is: **a person's mental concept of the "big picture" of reality, as shaped by conscious beliefs or subconscious assumptions about God, Creation, Mankind, Moral Order, and Purpose.**[3]

So I was coming to understand that at the very beginning of a person's worldview is the question, Is there a God? Everybody has to answer this question by faith. However you answer this question will determine how the other big questions about life will be answered. Questions like, Where did we come from? Did we evolve or were we created? Do I have a purpose? Is there a right and wrong, and who determines what is right or wrong? How a person answers those questions then determines much of how a person lives their life.

So at the very beginning of a worldview I see three possibilities: there is no

God, there is a God, or there are either many gods or all is god. Those three could be categorized in this way:

• Atheistic worldview—this would include humanism and Marxism
• Monotheistic worldview—this would include Christianity, Judaism, and Islam
• Pan/Polytheism—this would include Hinduism, animism, and New Age

So if a worldview is literally how people view their world, and there are at least three main categories of the way people view their world, I could already see the folly in the attitude that we should just all get along and coexist with one another. That advice was going to be harder to reckon with than one might think. I was going to need some help putting all this information together in a cogent manner.

GETTING MORE INFORMATION ON WORLDVIEWS

• • •

Back when I was first formulating the outline for this project, I knew right away that answering these arguments would require more firepower than I could generate on my own. If I was going to get in-depth answers, I needed to pick the brains of people I would consider to be experts in the subjects we wanted to discuss. So I placed some phone calls and send out some e-mails to inquire about the possibility of conducting face-to-face interviews with these experts in order to gain more understanding in these areas.

My first trip took me from my home base in Oklahoma City to the beautiful hamlet of Manitou Springs, Colorado. I flew to Denver, rented a car, and enjoyed a delightful drive just a little past Colorado Springs to my destination. While on the road, I drove past the U.S. Air Force Academy, and to my pleasant surprise, six of their fighter jets were flying in close and precise formation over the peaks of the Rocky Mountains. It was truly an unexpected pleasure!

My GPS guided me to the correct street address I needed in the tiny hamlet of Manitou Springs. This is the home of Summit Ministries. I smiled as I pulled up to the address, because it turned out to be a beautifully renovated hotel building that dates back to the 1890s. The clapboard siding gleams with creamy white paint trimmed with deep green. What immediately grabs your attention is the front porch, as wide as the hotel, framed in large white columns and long white railings and lined with tall green rocking chairs. I was hoping we could visit the front porch again, it was that inviting.

I was met at the front by the executive director of Summit Ministries, John Stonestreet. One of Summit's main thrusts is a two-week workshop on the subject of worldviews that is specifically geared for high school and college students. Upon my arrival, I discovered that John was in the middle of a two-week session, but he had graciously taken several hours out of his busy schedule to visit with me. Casual was the dress code for this conference, so John was dressed in jeans and a long sleeved shirt, with the sleeves comfortably rolled up. In his early thirties, John seems the perfect age to be young enough to relate to his target audience yet old enough to offer the voice of experience. Plus, once he flashes a wonderfully contagious smile, you're immediately won over.

After a brief tour of the grounds, John read my mind and said, "Why don't we go back out to the front porch and pull up a couple of those big rocking chairs? That would be a nice, quiet place for us to have our conversation."

I couldn't agree more. It was a flawless spring day in Colorado. The sun was shining brightly, and there was a gentle breeze moving ever so slightly. All signs pointed to an excellent setting for an interview.

"John, I think we should begin this conversation by establishing some common terms and some common ground. So, first of all, how would you define the term *worldview*?" I asked, curious to hear how his definition would compare to the one I had learned from Overman and Johnson.

John replied, "The definition I use when I speak on this subject, as well as the definition I've used in the books I've written is: *the framework of our most basic beliefs that shapes our view of and for the world and is the basis of our decisions and actions.* Everyone has basic beliefs about life. They shape the way we live and the decisions we make."

"And no matter what our worldview, some of those views are accepted by faith, correct?" I interjected.

"Precisely. Choosing to deny faith in a God is still an act of faith, since neither option cannot be absolutely proven. We have to evaluate which answer makes the most sense of life as we know it. So we begin by looking at the most important questions of life—what many call the ultimate questions."

"Can you describe the questions you're referring to?" I asked.

"Sure," John replied quite willingly. "Questions like: Where did everything come from? I'd call that *outward*. Another question—Is there a God? I describe that one as *upward*. A third area would be a question like—Is there right and wrong? I call this *inward*. These are the sorts of questions that all human beings wrestle with, whether they think about them or not. It's just part of being human."

John pressed on. "Allow me to return to the initial question concerning worldview. In its simplest terms, worldview is your view of the world based on how you answer those questions. You don't look *at* a worldview, you look *through* a worldview. I often use eyeglasses or contact lenses to illustrate what a worldview is all about. Once you are wearing glasses or contacts, you forget you have them on, but they affect your vision. Your worldview is the lens through which you see reality. It's how we orient ourselves to the world."

"So it's really where it all begins," I commented.

"That's correct, Steve," John replied. "It is the most fundamental thing about how we engage in the world. Actually I borrowed the lens metaphor from our founder here at Summit Ministries, Dr. David Noebel. We all call him 'Doc' around here. I have asked him to join us a little later, if that's okay with you."

"Not a problem," I replied. "I look forward to meeting him."

"Here's how Doc elaborates on the lens idea:

To say that a worldview is "an interpretive framework" is to say that a worldview is like a pair of glasses—it is something through which you view everything. And the fact is, everyone has a worldview, a way he or she looks at the world.

Have you ever put on someone else's glasses? If you have, than you know that they do not always help your sight. In fact, putting on someone else's glasses can give you a headache, a throbbing pain in your eyes, or simply make you dizzy. If the prescription for the glasses is not the right one for you, what you see through the glasses will be a distorted view of reality. In other words, without the proper prescription, glasses will not help you see the world clearly; rather they will keep you from seeing the world as it truly is.[4]

"So if we have the right worldview," I commented, "we can better see and understand the world around us, and if we have a wrong worldview, we will be at risk of wrong conclusions about life and the world around us."

"Exactly," John replied.

"To better understand the different worldviews," I said, "let's go back to your three groups and look at how they differ in their view of the upward, inward, and outward."

"I'll give you a word or phrase for all of them, and then I have a copy of my book here that I will give you so you can reproduce one of the charts in it for your own book. Let's first look at what you're calling atheism. In terms of their upward belief, they would say there is no God. Regarding outward—our origins—they believe in natural causes and processes or evolution. Their inward morality is human-centered, therefore relative."

"What about pan/polytheism?" I asked.

John replied, "As their upward view, they believe that God or the gods are just a part of the universe like we are. Outward, their understanding is that all things are part of the 'divine oneness.' And their inward belief is that we share in the divinity of all things. So, like humanism, morality is human-centered and therefore relative."

"That leaves monotheism," I added. "Can you sum them up in the same manner?"

"Upward is a belief in one God. Outward—their origin is explained by being created by God. Inward is a morality that is God-centered and therefore absolute.

"This is a very basic look at worldviews, and there are many variations of these three basic beliefs," John explained. "For example, there are those that are monotheistic who believe that God used evolutionary processes in the creation of the world. There are many possible combinations of worldviews, but these three can be used to further our discussion."

SO WHY CAN'T WE JUST COEXIST?

. . .

It was at this point that I decided to move closer to the first group of complaints that we had received. "So, John, whether we chose three or many different types of worldviews, the question I've been asked is why we can't all just get along with one another? Why can't we coexist?"

"People have always struggled with the notion that there are many 'religions.' It's called pluralism, and it leaves many with an uncomfortable feeling." John replied. "This whole idea of coexisting implies that when it comes to our worldview, what we believe is nothing but an opinion. It's not really true, so we shouldn't offend anyone with our beliefs. But it is an issue of truth. Either God exists or He does not. And it's a truth that really matters one way or the other. Imagine if we lived out this coexistence mind-set with other things. For example, if you're house is on fire, and I see it, I'd yell at the top of my lungs, 'YOUR HOUSE IS ON FIRE!!!' But if you yell back, 'NO, IT'S NOT.' What should I do? Should I say nothing more because I do not want to be intolerant? Should I watch your house burn to the ground? No! Because this issue really matters! Someone is right and someone is wrong. The problem with coexisting is that two opposing truth claims cannot both be true.

"I believe that the question of whether or not God exists is the central question one must answer. If He does exist, who is He and what does He ask of us? G. K. Chesterton said that if a man will not believe in God, the danger is not that he will believe in nothing, but that he will believe in anything.

"We can't 'just coexist,' because we are dealing with questions regarding the ultimate truths of reality. Either God exists or not. There is a wonderful quote attributed to H. G. Wells that goes something like: 'If there is no God, nothing matters. If there is a God, nothing else matters.'

"In my book I write about this subject, and I once again refer to the

Across the manger of Bethlehem lay the shadow of the cross.

FOR TO US A CHILD IS BORN, TO US A SON IS GIVEN,
AND THE GOVERNMENT WILL BE ON HIS SHOULDERS...

- ISAIAH 9:6 NIV

metaphor of worldviews as eyeglasses or contact lenses. Here's how I say it in one of the early chapters:

> A worldview can function as a pair of glasses through which we observe and understand our world. Everything we perceive must come through these glasses. If such glasses have "Christian" lenses, then everything we observe will be "tinted" Christian. We will explain the universe and life's events from a Christian perspective. We will not understand why others do not see the world as we do—it is so obvious to us.
>
> The same is true for those who wear atheist glasses or Buddhist glasses. They will "see" the same world, but it will be understood differently. Their "glasses" (worldview) do not shape reality nor do they ensure a correct perception, but they do determine a person's **explanation and interpretation** of life and the world.
>
> A biblical worldview is thus a perspective that sees everything through the "glasses" of Scripture. Rather than allowing culture or experience to determine a worldview, it allows the Bible to make the determination.[5]

John was on a roll, and I was nodding in hearty agreement. It was at that point that a distinguished older man walked onto the front porch, and I quickly concluded that this must be David Noebel. Doc was dressed in a conservative business suit, dress shirt, and necktie. While we shook hands, he explained that he had just come from a radio interview in Colorado Springs, where he had the opportunity to introduce more people to the mission of Summit Ministries. Doc is in his seventies, looks fabulous for his age, and it has to have something to do with the fact that he is surrounded by high school and college students almost all the time.

"Doc, we're talking about why our worldviews make it so that we can't just coexist with one another," John jumped in, attempting to bring Doc up to speed with our discussion.

"Ah, yes, coexistence and the plea for tolerance," Doc mused. "Have you ever noticed that those calling for tolerance are themselves not being tolerant?"

"That's an interesting observation," I pondered. "The accuser is guilty of the accusation?"

"Absolutely. They are yelling 'tolerance' because they are disagreeing with another person's position."

"Plus tolerance, when defined this way, neuters debate." John interjected, "It's no longer appropriate to discuss the truth claims of different belief systems. We have to pretend that they don't make any truth claims at all."

TRUTH: INCLUSIVE OR EXCLUSIVE?

• • •

"Josh McDowell has a great illustration in his book *Evidence That Demands a Verdict*," Doc added. "You know the one to which I'm referring—right John? The Washington, D.C. analogy."

"Let me grab a copy of that book for you," John volunteered. "I know exactly where it is in the book." In a flash John was back with McDowell's book. He opened it up to one of the early pages and read aloud the following analogy:

> Why can't you [Christians] accept other people and what they believe as also true?… This misconception assumes that truth is inclusive, that it gathers under its wings claims that oppose each other. The fact, however, is that all truth is exclusive—at least to some degree—for it must exclude as false that which is not true.
>
> For instance, it is true that Washington, D.C. is the capital city of the United States of America. This means that no other city in the United States is that country's capital. In fact, no other city on planet Earth or anywhere in the universe can lay legitimate claim to being the capital city of the United States. One city and one only fits the bill, and that's Washington, D.C.
>
> Simply because just one city is the United States capital does not mean that the people who affirm this truth are therefore intolerant. They may like scores of other cities and even live in different cities themselves.

They may even live in different countries and prefer their country to America. Accepting the exclusive truth claim about Washington, D.C. does not make a person tolerant or intolerant—it simply makes him or her correct about what the capital city of the United States is.

The same is true about Christianity. If the claims of the Christian faith are true—and many people accept them as true—these people are no more intolerant for their belief than those people who accept Washington, D.C. as the United States capital. They are either correct or mistaken about how God revealed Himself in the world. If they are right, then there really is no other way to God but through Christ. If they are wrong, then Christianity is false. The question of tolerance isn't the issue. The question of **truth** is.[6]

"So if someone takes seriously the whole idea of worldviews, they will see that it isn't really possible to just coexist and get along. Our worldview will require us to see things differently," I volunteered as John finished reading. "Truth isn't inclusive, it's exclusive."

I continued. "The implication of how a society answers the question, Is there a God? becomes significant. Every country in the world has a predominant worldview its government is built around. The laws of a country are reflective of the predominant worldview of the country. The laws of Iran are different from the laws of Russia, which are different from the laws of England. Many of the differences could be explained by the different worldviews of each country. A person from Iran going to Russia and wanting to live there based on the laws of Iran would have a problem no different from a person from England going to Iran or a person going from Russia to England."

"We're not saying that people should be antagonistic about different worldviews," Doc added, "but we are saying it's a bit naive to believe that we can all hold our own worldviews while coexisting in some inclusive group. The truth won't allow us."

It was that last statement that I found fascinating. "What do you mean by an inclusive group, and what is the problem that an inclusive group presents?" I asked.

"A society can no more coexist with different worldviews any more than drivers can decide to make up their own traffic rules to live by without having chaos!" I stated. "If a person moves to America from England, he may have learned to drive on the left side of the road, but in our country he is going to have a problem if he doesn't agree to do it our way!"

John added, "It really matters what you mean by the word 'coexist.' We can coexist if that means recognizing and respecting each person's eternal worth and dignity. But we can't all believe anything and everything. That would be throwing ideologies together in such a way that it would neuter the beliefs. Homosexuality and Islam cannot coexist. They each are based in worldviews that oppose the other."

"It seems like the big question is, Which worldview gets to determine which beliefs we live by," I commented.

"I can think of two examples of how that question plays out," John replied. "We would consider one of these examples positive and the other negative."

"What are the examples?" I asked.

"Consider the moment in time in the history of the United States when the territory of Utah was about to become a state in the Union. Prior to statehood, the Mormon Church encouraged polygamy. It wasn't until the church changed its teaching that Utah was allowed to become a state. Coexisting was not an option. Someone had to change.

"Plus, when you think about it, people are being 'left out' of marriage all the time!" he continued. "Polygamists are left out. Homosexuals are left out. Men who want to marry animals are left out. It's the way our law is structured."

"Okay, polygamy in Utah is a good example of worldviews colliding in a group dynamic," I summed up. "What's the other example that you have?"

"Catholic Charities of Washington D.C. was forced to end its adoptive programs because it would not agree to provide adoptions for same sex marriages, which became the law in the District of Columbia in early 2010," John replied. "They were basically forced out of business because they could not coexist.

They issued a statement that said, in part: 'Although Catholic Charities has an 80 year legacy of high quality service to the vulnerable in our nation's capital, the D.C. government informed Catholic Charities that the agency would be ineligible to serve as a foster care provider due to the impending D.C. same sex marriage law.'"[7]

"Those are two powerful examples of the inability of different worldviews to coexist," I commented.

Without realizing it, we had used up all our time. John had an open forum to conduct with the students there on campus, and Doc was scheduled for a ninety-minute lecture after the forum. Graciously, the two men invited me to stay and attend both meetings, which I did. What a wonderful outreach to a generation so hungry for the truth!

It was my understanding that our forefathers built our society around the Judeo-Christian, biblical worldview. Was America truly founded as a Christian nation? That would be the next issue I would need to track down with an expert. •

You choose your beliefs,

your neatly tied package of what can
and cannot be. With these beliefs we
weave the fabric of our religion.

But *what if* God refuses to be defined
by what we consider believable?
What if truth is not
something we create,
but something we discover,
and embrace?

What if God is actively and
aggressively looking for you?
What if He really desires to
spend eternity with you?

What if
He rose
from the dead
to prove it?

"Seek the Lord while He may be found; call on Him while He is near.
Let the wicked forsake his way and the evil man his thoughts.
Let him turn to the Lord, and He will have mercy on him,
And to our God, for He will freely pardon."
- Isaiah 55:6-7

5

SEPARATION OF CHURCH AND STATE

The second general area of criticism in the letters we received as a result of the Hobby Lobby Fourth of July ad was from writers who took a neutral position on religion. The letters alluded to the separation of church and state. Though Hobby Lobby is neither a church nor a state, the argument is that a business should not have a religion any more than a school or a government. They also questioned the idea that we were founded as a Christian nation, which many of the quotes indicate. Historically, they reasoned, the Founding Fathers never intended for us to be viewed as a Christian nation, which is why they instigated the separation of church and state. These complaints did not argue that religion was either good or bad; they just felt that a business shouldn't have a position on religion.

This argument is a common one. Much of the basis for the argument rests on a flawed understanding of what was really going on in the minds of the Founding Fathers more than two hundred years ago. If we could somehow get into their heads, we would have a much better appreciation for the meanings of their words and the context behind them. And I knew just the person who could help me do that exact thing.

Tucked away in a tiny Texas town about forty-five minutes west of Fort Worth is the person who arguably has one of the deepest modern understandings of what was going on in the minds of the Founding Fathers when they formed our nation over two centuries ago. David Barton is the founder and president of an organization called Wallbuilders. David had originally helped us come up with the quotes that we used in our Fourth of July ad. I decided that a trip to Fort Worth was necessary to get answers to my questions from David. He graciously consented to my interview request, so I showed up at his office at nine o'clock one bright, crisp Monday morning in March.

Wallbuilders is an organization dedicated to presenting America's forgotten history and heroes with an emphasis on our moral, religious, and constitutional heritage. As its founder, David has written numerous best-selling works as well as being a national award-winning historian who brings a fresh and accurate perspective to history.

It was such a delight to have a few hours with him. After I had a brief tour of his facility, including a library containing an amazing collection of books, letters, and other documents primarily from the period in our history prior to 1812, we settled into a spacious conference room and began our discussion.

ARE WE A REPUBLIC OR A THEOCRACY?
. . .

"Some of the folks that wrote to us felt that the quotes we used in our Fourth of July ad suggested a theocracy, like what you find in Iran."

Leaning forward in his seat, David responded. "Historically, a theocracy has always been implemented in order to instill fear. In order for the United States to be a theocracy, you'd have to demolish our Constitution. A theocracy limits votes whereas our republic provides the opportunity and privilege for all to vote.

"A republic is a representative form of government," David continued. "Our forefathers got the idea straight from the Bible. The children of Israel are an example of both the separation of church and state and a representative from of government. Moses and Aaron were put over separate institutions; Moses over civil affairs and Aaron over the temple affairs. And they were also told to pick leaders from among themselves. American Christian leaders were well aware of the theocracies that certain monarchs had created earlier in European history, and they resoundingly denounced that model as *not* being representative of a true Christian nation. For example, consider Noah Webster. He was a veteran of the Revolutionary War, a legislator, and a judge. He said, "The ecclesiastical establishments of Europe which serve to support tyrannical governments are not the Christian religion, but abuses and corruptions of it."[8] He was pointing out that a tyrannical or coercive Christian religion is not truly Christian!

Daniel Webster also asserted that Christianity as practiced in America was dramatically different from Christianity as it had been practiced in Europe. He described American Christianity as "Christianity to which the sword and the fagot [a burning stake or a hot branding iron] are unknown—general tolerant Christianity is the law of the land!"[9]

"We just weren't set up to force our faith on anybody who didn't want it," David continued. "The fact that European countries were experiencing monarchs who were mandating religion was part of the motivation for our Founding Fathers to set forth our government in the exact opposite manner. In the words of Thomas Jefferson: 'The comparisons of our governments with those of Europe are like a comparison of heaven and hell.'"[10]

WHAT ABOUT THE PHRASE "SEPARATION OF CHURCH AND STATE"?

· · ·

I asked, "Since the U.S. Constitution does not mention God, and the First Amendment says that Congress shall make no law respecting an establishment of religion, how can our forefathers claim this to be a Christian nation? Wasn't the separation of church and state what the forefathers were after to prevent our country from becoming the intolerant state they were fleeing?"

"Exactly, Steve," David agreed. "By the way, many people assume that it was Thomas Jefferson who first developed the phrase and the concept of the 'wall of separation' between church and state, but the principle was actually espoused by biblically oriented Christian leaders as early as the late 1500s during the English Reformation period. By the early 1600s the concept had already been implanted deeply on this continent by American clergymen as well."

"So Jefferson is not the one who coined the phrase?" I repeated.

"That's correct. But he wanted it to be clearly understood, because at the time the state had a nasty habit of working its way into the church, not the church working its way into the state," he replied.

"When the state officially recognized the Christian church as its official religion, this led to the state's becoming coercive, dictating all to be Christian. This led to many abuses and is what the Reformation recognized as a problem when the church and the state become one. The state tried to keep the Scriptures from the common man, which led to abuses like the Inquisition and parts of the Crusades.

"In his second inaugural address, Jefferson said, 'In matters of religion I have considered that its free exercise is placed by the Constitution independent of the powers of the general [federal] government.'[11]

"Three years later, in a letter to Justice Samuel Miller, Jefferson reinforced his position: 'I consider the government of the United States as interdicted [prohibited] by the Constitution from intermeddling with religious institutions...or exercises.'[12]

"So the First Amendment was not pointed at a citizen's religious beliefs or expressions, whether practiced in private or public, but at the impropriety of the state's dictating those beliefs or, limiting those expressions. The First Amendment was a restriction on government, not on citizens," David concluded with confidence.

WHAT IS MEANT BY THE TERM "CHRISTIAN NATION"?

• • •

"David, if our forefathers were not wanting a theocracy and were establishing a separation of church and state, it appears they were wanting a secular state," I said. "How could they claim America was a Christian nation?"

"First of all," he answered, "it might be helpful to understand what is *not* meant by the words 'Christian nation.' As I have written in my book, it doesn't mean all citizens are Christians. Nor does it mean that the law requires everyone to adhere to some sort of Christian theology. Furthermore, it does not mean that all our leaders are Christians."

"Okay, I've got a better understanding of what is not meant by those words," I responded. "So what do we mean when we say we're a Christian nation?"

"Justice David Brewer, a justice on the U.S. Supreme Court a hundred years ago, made a succinct statement that still carries weight to this day:

> [In] what sense can [America] be called a Christian nation? Not in the sense that Christianity is the established religion or that the people are in any manner compelled to support it. On the contrary, the Constitution specifically provides that 'Congress shall make no law respecting an establishment of religion, or prohibiting the free exercise thereof.' Neither is it Christian in the sense that all its citizens are either in fact or name Christians. On the contrary, all religions have free scope within our borders.
>
> Numbers of our people profess other religions, and may reject all. Nor is it Christian in the sense that a profession of Christianity is a condition of holding office or otherwise engaging in public service, or essential to recognition either politically or socially. In fact the government as a legal organization is independent of all religions. Nevertheless, we constantly speak of this republic as a Christian nation—in fact, as the leading Christian nation in the world.[13]

At that point David paused. I was hooked. "Okay," I said, "it is clear again what is *not* meant by the terms 'Christian nation.' But does Justice Brewer articulate what does allow us to make that claim?"

"Yes, he does," David replied. "Later in the document Justice Brewer states that America was 'of all nations of the world...most justly called a Christian nation [because Christianity] has so largely shaped and molded it.'[14]

By definition then, a Christian nation is a nation founded upon Christian and biblical principles whose society and institutions are shaped by those principles. And scores of court cases affirm that America is a Christian nation."

I continued with my questions. "In what way has Christianity molded and shaped our nation?"

"Well, just to name a few, our republican form of government is a biblical concept starting when Moses instructed the people to pick leaders from among themselves, as recorded in Exodus 18:21. Also, America was the first to champion and enshrine into their governing documents the rights of religious toleration and protection for conscience that had been reintroduced by the Reformers and which are mentioned several dozen times in the New Testament. It made America the world's single greatest historical force in securing noncoercion, religious toleration, and the rights of conscience—all Christian concepts! As Noah Webster affirmed:

> Where will you find any codes of laws among civilized men in which the commands and prohibitions are not founded on Christian principles? I need not specify the prohibition of murder, robbery, theft, trespass; but commercial and social regulations are all derived from those principles, or intended to enforce them. The laws of contracts and bills of exchange are founded on the principles of justice, the basis of all security of rights in society. The laws of insurance are founded on the Christian principle of benevolence, and intended to protect men from want and distress. The provisions of law for the relief of the poor are in pursuance of Christian principles. Every wise code of laws must embrace the main principles of the religion of Christ.[15]

"Webster had even more to say about the subject. For example, 'The brief exposition of the Constitution of the United States will unfold to young persons the principles of republican government; and…that the genuine source of correct republican principles, is the Bible, particularly the New Testament or the Christian religion.'[16]

"Brewer and Webster are not the only individuals who saw us that way. So many of our presidents also have embraced the concept of America being a Christian nation," David continued.

"Do you have a few examples?" I asked.

"Yes, I do," he responded with a chuckle. "You already quoted several of them in your Fourth of July ad, but here are a few more for your consideration. At George Washington's inauguration, he underscored his belief in his Christian heritage and paid homage to our heavenly Father by saying: 'It would be particularly improper in this first official act my fervent supplications to that Almighty Being Who rules over the universe, Who presides in the council of nations, and Whose providential aids can supply every human defect—that His benediction may consecrate to the liberties and happiness of the people of the United States a government instituted by themselves for these essential purposes.'[17]

"John Adams said it this way: 'The general principles on which the fathers achieved independence were...the general principles of Christianity.'[18]

"There are numerous examples of Thomas Jefferson's referring to the United States as a Christian nation, if one examines his writings—one of them you include in your ad," David pressed on. "I'll give you a reference you can footnote for your readers to check out."[19]

"Consider this quote from President James Madison, delivered at the conclusion of the War of 1812. It's from a document I have in my personal collection: 'No people ought to feel greater obligations to celebrate the goodness of the Great Disposer of Events and of the Destiny of Nations than the people of the United States.... And to that same Divine Author of Every Good and Perfect Gift (James 1:17) we are indebted for all those privileges and advantages, religious as well as civil, which are so richly enjoyed in this favored land.'[20]

"I can go on and on," David volunteered. "John Quincy Adams, Andrew Jackson, John Tyler, Zachary Taylor, James Buchanan, Abraham Lincoln, U. S. Grant, James Garfield, William McKinley, Theodore Roosevelt, Woodrow Wilson, Herbert Hoover, Franklin Roosevelt, Dwight Eisenhower, Richard Nixon, and Ronald Reagan—and these are just some of our presidents. I could list many, many more. The point to be made is that even our commanders in chief were firmly convinced that ours was a Christian nation, knowing that it was Christian principles that were used to shape our society."

WHAT ABOUT THE TREATY OF TRIPOLI?

• • •

I recalled some of the other letters we received and decided to address another topic with David. "It seems whenever we have a discussion of this nature, we are accused of taking our forefathers out of context, then someone always brings up the Treaty of Tripoli, signed by President John Adams. Didn't the Treaty of Tripoli claim we were not a Christian nation?"

David took a sip of his iced tea and then returned in earnest to our conversation. "I'll give you the bottom line first and then I'll explain. Taking a closer look at the Treaty of Tripoli reveals that the statement in question is really only a portion of the statement that was made—so it's a misquote out of context. Second, the statement in question is a note added by a secretary in a bumbling attempt to clarify what is being said!"

"Can you explain?" I asked.

"The Treaty with Tripoli was one of the many treaties negotiated during the Barbary Wars against Muslim terrorists that began at the end of our Revolutionary War and continued on through the presidencies of Washington, Adams, Jefferson, and Madison. Five Muslim countries—Algiers, Morocco, Tunis, Turkey, and Tripoli—made indiscriminate attacks against the property and interests of what they claimed to be 'Christian nations'—countries like England, France, Spain, Denmark, Sweden, and many others, including the United States. The conflict escalated to the point that Tripoli in 1801 declared war against the United States, which, by the way, was young America's first official war since being established as a nation.

"As an example, in one month in the year 1793, Algiers alone seized ten American ships, enslaving more than one hundred sailors, and holding them for sale or for ransom. Our government did all it could to establish peace with these Muslim nations, constantly reassuring them that, as Christians, we meant no harm to them as Muslims. In treaty after treaty, we used multiple phrases and clauses to demonstrate that America was *not* like some so-called European Christian nations earlier in history that had attacked others simply because they were Muslims. No, it was just the opposite!

"The 1797 treaty was just one of the many treaties in which each country recognized the religion of the other country and in which America invoked rhetoric designed to reassure Muslim nations that we had no interest in going to war with them over religious principles. Article 11 of the treaty reads as follows:

> As the Government of the United States of America is not in any sense founded on the Christian religion as it has in itself no character of enmity against the laws, religion, or tranquility of Musselman [Muslims] and as the said States [America] have never entered into any war or act of hostility against any Mahometan nation, it is declared by the parties that no pretext arising from religious opinions shall ever produce an interruption of the harmony existing between the two countries.[21]

"Notice, Steve, that article 11 is actually eighty-three words long, but critics amazingly place a period right in the middle of a sentence—a location where no punctuation existed, thus stopping the sentence in midthought after only nineteen words! Doing so is an attempt at reversing the meaning. But when you read the article in its entirety, and its thought concludes where the punctuation so indicates, then the article simply assures Muslims at Tripoli that we were not one of the Christian nations with an inherent hostility against Muslims and that, for our part, we would not allow differences in 'religious opinions' to lead to hostility."

I shook my head in disbelief. "So in reality one of the main quotes critics use against America as a Christian nation was, in fact, taken out of context—making the accuser guilty of the accusation!"

"That's right," David nodded. "And incidentally, here's another interesting fact about that particular treaty. Originally, the treaty was written in Arabic, then translated into Italian, then translated into English from the Italian translation by a diplomat named Joel Barlow. Barlow's translation is extremely faulty, so much so that the U.S. State Department has announced that *there is actually no article 11 in the original treaty!*"

WHAT ABOUT QUOTES THAT SAY JUST THE OPPOSITE?
. . .

"There were folks who responded to our advertisement with the sentiment that said something to the effect that for every quote listed there is another one from the same person indicating just the opposite of what we printed. How do you respond to a statement of that nature?"

"Since we just talked about John Adams, let's look at him a little bit more," David responded. "He is a favorite target of this sort of tactic. One of the more famous antireligious quotes attributed to John Adams is the statement, 'This would be the best of all possible worlds if there were no religion in it.'"

"Yes, I have actually heard people use that quote as a retort concerning John Adams having any sort of faith whatsoever," I volunteered.

"Adams did in fact make that statement," David replied to my complete shock. Before I could raise my surprise, however, he continued. "But it is another statement that is taken out of context and therefore distorted. The quote comes from a letter Adams wrote to Thomas Jefferson on April 19, 1817. The point that he was making was that Christians often are intolerant of one another in their various denominations. To illustrate his point, he vividly recalls a conversation between two ministers that he had witnessed many years before:

> Seventy years ago...Lemuel Bryant was my parish priest and Joseph Cleverly my Latin schoolmaster. Lemuel was a jocular and liberal scholar and divine. Joseph a scholar and a gentleman.... The parson and the pedagogue lived much together, but were eternally disputing about government and religion. One day when the schoolmaster had been more than commonly fanatical and declared "If he were a monarch, he would have but one religion in his dominions" the parson coolly replied, "Cleverly! You would be the best man in the world if you had no religion."

"But listen to Adam's opinion on this issue, detailed later in the same letter:

Twenty times in the course of my late reading I have been on the point of breaking out, "This would be the best of all possible worlds if there were no religion in it!!!" But in this exclamation I would have been as fanatical as Bryant or Cleverly. Without religion this world would be something not fit to be mentioned in polite company, I mean hell.[22]

"So Adams's position on religion is exactly the opposite of what the critics suggest. He was saying that it would be 'fanatical' to consider a world without religion, and furthermore that world could only be described as 'hell.'"

"That's truly amazing," I replied.

"By the way," David smiled and leaned in for effect. "Jefferson wrote him back two weeks later and agreed!"[23]

WHAT ABOUT THE SUPREME COURT CASE WE QUOTED?

. . .

"Okay," I said. "Let's turn our attention to one of the Supreme Court cases that we quoted in the ad. *Vidal v. Girard's Executors*, 1844. Some of our readers felt that we had taken the quotes out of context. Would you care to comment on that claim?"

"Well, there is no way to make a case for the quote in your ad to be seen as taken out of context," David began. "The case to which you refer centered around the issue of whether or not government-assisted schools could provide religious exercises during their school day. Defending the right for the teaching of the Scriptures was none other than the famous orator and statesman Daniel Webster. A member of the House of Representatives for ten years, a member of the U.S. Senate for nineteen years, and secretary of state for no less than *three* presidents, Webster was one of the most influential politicians of his day. Among his many wonderful arguments in this landmark case was this magnificent quote: 'It will therefore, soothe the heart of no Christian parent...that [his children] may be...shut up through the most interesting period of their lives in a [school] without religion."[24]

"Daniel Webster was not alone in his belief," David continued. "As a matter of fact, the Supreme Court handed down a unanimous decision requiring that government-assisted schools provide opportunities for religious exercises. So the quote in your ad was right on, Steve."

"I thought so," I replied. "So, once again, we were correct in using the quote from that Supreme Court ruling. It truly does affirm that biblical exposure in a public educational setting was supported by the Supreme Court."

"That is exactly what the ruling affirmed," David replied.

"Times have changed, haven't they?" I lamented.

"Yes, it's sad but true," David replied. "But you may be interested in knowing," he added, "there are also Supreme Court Cases from 1943 and 1963 that similarly affirm keeping religion in public schools. For example, in the 1943 decision of *Murdock v. Pennsylvania,* the Court said, 'Freedom of religion [is] available to all, not merely those who can pay their own way.'"[25]

FINAL THOUGHTS
. . .

"David, this time together has been incredibly informative," I said as I glanced at my watch, realizing our allotted time was just about expired.

"It is my pleasure," David replied. "As you can probably tell, these matters are a real passion of mine. I really want folks to understand the incredible spiritual beliefs that our Founding Fathers embraced."

"The United States of America truly is a great nation," I concluded. "It's a place with exceptional opportunity." I paused for a moment to allow that thought to sink in. "Do you agree, David?"

"Yes, without question," he replied.

The spiritual beliefs that David refers to are what made up their worldview. It was the Christian worldview that "has so strongly shaped and molded" America's founding. •

"This is a Christian Nation. More than a half century ago that declaration was written into the decrees of the highest court in this land."

PRESIDENT HARRY TRUMAN[26]

.

"Of the many influences that have shaped the United States of America into a distinctive Nation and people, none may be said to be more fundamental and enduring than the Bible."

PRESIDENT RONALD REAGAN[27]

BECAUSE HE LIVES YOU CAN HAVE ETERNAL LIFE

If you confess with your mouth the Lord Jesus, and believe in your heart that
God has raised Him from the dead, you shall have eternal life.
-paraphrased from Romans 10:9

6

ALL RELIGIONS ARE BAD

We've looked at the first two complaints raised against our ad: (1) all religions are good, so we should just all get along and coexist, and (2) the more neutral position of the need for a strict separation between church and state. The third category of complaint falls under the heading of all religions are bad and would come from an atheistic perspective. To better understand this argument, it is necessary to understand the atheistic worldview. This worldview goes hand in hand with the theory of evolution. Since there is no God, an atheist would argue, we have evolved into what we are today, and "religion" would do well to leave us alone. As one of the letters to us stated: "Nations led by fundamentalist extremists, no matter what faith they embrace, have always been the source of profound human suffering. Always."

While this writer is primarily concerned with "fundamentalist extremists" of any faith, I would have to imagine that, in a perfect world for him, there would be no faith at all, not even a moderate faith. While there are many atrocities have been committed in the name of faith, what I had come to understand was that the worst atrocities could be attributed to a worldview of no faith or, rather, an atheistic faith.

When I was in Texas to interview David Barton for the preceding chapter, as a passing thought, he mentioned the following statistics in order to put some history into its proper perspective:

- Christians have been blamed for twenty million deaths in twenty centuries.
- Adolf Hitler is personally responsible for the deaths of thirteen million.
- Communism is responsible for one hundred million deaths in the twentieth century alone!

One cannot argue with the numbers presented in those statements.

Another letter to us said, "It is imperative that everyone abandon 'faith' in favor of learning, evidence and knowledge."

Here, again, the writer is assuming that no faith is possible. But a belief in no God *is* a faith claim. One cannot prove that there is no God. If you can't prove there is a God, and you can't prove there isn't a God, the question becomes, Where does the evidence lead? A person of faith shouldn't be afraid of "learning, evidence and knowledge," because if he is right, the evidence should support his faith. So where does the evidence lead? The theory of evolution is so widely accepted, isn't that where all the evidence leads?

To get some answers I turned to Ken Ham, CEO of Answers in Genesis Ministry and the Creation Museum, who I knew had spent the greater part of his life pursuing the evidence of creation and evolution. Ken's schooling occurred in his native Australia. He has a bachelor's degree in applied science with an emphasis on environmental biology from Queensland Institute of Technology as well as a diploma of education from the University of Queensland. In the United States, Ken has been awarded three honorary doctorates. He has written numerous books and articles on creation versus evolution and has defended the biblical position on such television shows as *The O'Reilly Factor, Fox and Friends, The Situation Room with Wolf Blitzer, Good Morning America, The NBC Nightly News with Brian Williams,* and *The PBS News Hour with Jim Lehrer.*

I arranged to visit with Ken at his office in the Creation Museum near Cincinnati, Ohio, conveniently situated near the airport. I flew in the night before and woke up the next morning to a light rain. After a short drive down the freeway, I was at the main entrance to the museum. Ken and some of his staff greeted me warmly and ushered me inside.

Ken still has a distinctive Australian accent. Tall, slender, with steely eyes and a closely cropped graying beard, he is a man who is passionate about the teachings of the Bible and especially the first book of the Bible, Genesis.

After a brief tour of the museum, we settled into comfortable chairs in his office to discuss the issues on my mind. "Ken," I began, "the theory of evolution has been around for a while and seems to be pretty entrenched in the scientific community. What I have come to understand is that there are some serious questions about the theory, and that some argue for what is called intelligent design—the idea that there must have been an intelligence that designed all of life. If that is the case, why is evolution embraced to the degree that it is?"

THE SUPERNATURAL
. . .

"The answer is a simple one, but a sad one," Ken lamented. "*The starting point has changed.* We used to start with the supernatural, but scientists have replaced it with the natural. And of course, that leaves God out. There's a powerful scene in the recent movie made about Darwin, where one of his co-workers utters contemptuously, 'You've killed God, sir!' Freedom *of* religion has become freedom *from* religion. Without God, who ultimately determines what is right and what is wrong? Not acknowledging God is refusing to admit the supernatural."

"Isn't that the closed-minded position?" I countered. "No matter what the evidence indicates we will not accept the supernatural?"

Ken nodded in silent agreement.

"I have been told that science is what can be studied in a laboratory—that would exclude the supernatural, wouldn't it?"

"Yes," Ken replied, "but if science is as narrowly defined as you have heard,

then the origin of life is outside the sphere of science since it can't be reproduced. But science can include ideas that can't be proven with evidence to support or deny the idea."

EVOLUTION: WHAT'S TRUE AND WHAT'S NOT?

· · ·

I asked, "What would you say to a young high school or college student who
gets regular and routine bombardments concerning evolution as the truth and
creation as a lie?"

Ken sat back in his chair, crossed his long legs, and began an answer I'm
sure he has given hundreds if not thousands of times. "First of all, we need to
define evolution. If you look it up in the dictionary, it's defined as 'change.' But
Steve, what you are talking about is a much more specific use of the word. We
are talking about molecules-to-man evolution, the idea that all of life began at
the molecular level and evolved over time to all of life that we see today, even
mankind. It is the belief held by Charles Darwin, as stated in his book *The Origin
of Species,* so we also refer to it as Darwinian evolution."

"Okay, that's a helpful clarification," I interjected. "So I offer you the same
question, specifically concerning molecules-to-man evolution."

"The fundamental flaw of molecules-to-man evolution," Ken replied, "is that
it requires *new information* to form a new kind. Not just a new species within a
kind. but evolution from one kind to another. That is something that has never
been discovered or proven."

"What do you mean by 'new information would be needed'?" I asked.

"Let's look at cats. Today there are lots of different cats, but they're all still
cats. There are lots of different dogs, but they're still dogs. Cats can't become a
totally different kind of dog, because they don't possess the information necessary to make that transformation. A reptile becoming a bird is impossible,
because a reptile doesn't have the information to grow feathers. It's the same reason an apelike ancestor cannot become a man."

"I've heard it argued that the finch's beak is an example of evolution," I offered. "The argument is that the finch developed a longer beak during dry weather. How do you respond to that issue?"

"Big beaks and little beaks are just a rearrangement of the information in the gene pool. But that is a far cry from a reptile becoming a finch. Nothing has ever had that kind of ability."

UNDERSTANDING THE TERM "INFORMATION"
• • •

"So what do you mean when you use the term 'information'?"

"This is how my friend and colleague Mike Riddle clarifies the distinction between how an evolutionist and a creationist view the subject of information." Ken grabbed a book off his desk, opened to a page earmarked for our discussion, and read out loud the following:

> The importance of information to the creation/evolution debate is founded in the presuppositions of each model. The presupposition of the evolutionary model is materialism, which is the idea that everything in the universe is solely comprised of matter [mass and energy]. From this foundational assumption, evolutionists logically conclude that cosmic evolution, chemical evolution, and biological evolution are all true. The presupposition of materialism has been shown to be scientifically false.
>
> The presupposition of the Bible is that there is a God who created the universe, the earth, and all living organisms living on earth. This has been shown to be consistent with scientific discoveries that there is a non-material third fundamental entity called **information** that originates only from an intelligent source. The universe consists of more than just mass and energy, and the information found within the DNA system of all life originated from an all-knowing, all-powerful Creator God.[28]

"I have heard that the information from DNA is the most densely packed assembly of information in the known universe," I said.

"That's right," Ken answered. "And the information is a nonmaterial fundamental entity and cannot originate from purely material qualities. We believe that the source of this information has to be from a 'designer.'"

"Interesting," I thought aloud.

"It would be logical at this point for an evolutionist to bring up the whole area of *mutations,* which are defined as primarily permanent changes in the DNA strand. Evolutionists would say that over millions of years, increases in information caused by mutations, plus natural selection and other mechanisms, developed all the life forms we see on earth today.

"The problem facing the molecules-to-man evolutionist is that for a single-cell life form to give rise to a more advanced life form, there needs to be a gain in *new* information within the organism's genetic material. So for an amoeba, which is a single-cell organism, to evolve into something like a horse, new information would need to develop over time that would code for ears, lungs, brains, legs, etc. If the cell were to make a change like this, the DNA would need to mutate new information. And it would require billions of mutations in order to gain all the information necessary for this sort of evolution. The fact is, we don't observe this in nature. It's just the opposite. Organisms lose or maintain information."

"If mutations have shown not to produce new information, that presents a real fundamental flaw in molecules-to-man evolution." I observed.

"I picked up a science textbook from one of the major publishers at a local high school," I said to Ken. "I looked at the portion of the book that dealt with evolution, and there were three sections:

- Section 1: History of Evolutionary Thought
- Section 2: Evidence of Evolution
- Section 3: Evolution in Action

"If evolution has its flaws, why isn't there a section entitled 'Evidence Against Evolution'?"

"That just shows you the bias in the scientific community regarding evolution," Ken answered.

"Ben Stein made that point very well in his documentary *Expelled*." I added. "He points out that at the college level, professors who question the theory of evolution can lose funding, tenure, or even their jobs."

"But," Ken said, "I think something that a lot of people don't understand is that those of us who believe the biblical account of creation also *agree* with evolutionists on a number of key issues."

That comment surprised me. "What do we agree on?" I inquired.

"The biggie is what is known as *natural selection.*"

I was shocked to hear those words coming out of his mouth! "Natural selection?" I gasped. "I thought natural selection was synonymous with evolution!"

"You're not alone, Steve," Ken reassured me. "Many folks, including good Christians, think the two terms mean the same thing. But they don't. I've talked to so many people who think there's so much about natural selection that makes sense—so they can't understand why it's rejected by creationists. What a relief we provide when we tell them they're right! We accept natural selection as a part of God's plan in a cursed world; we just don't give it credit for what it can't do.

"Richard Dawkins is an atheistic professor at Oxford University, and he argues in his book *The God Delusion* that natural selection is the process of evolution. He points out that creationists argue that life is too complex to have just appeared as we see it today, and that the 'chance' of life is so improbable that there must have been a designer. He agrees that chance isn't a good answer for life, but he argues that natural selection is the answer. He says that natural selection gets you to the complexity of life one step at a time. Here is how he puts it in his book:

> What is it that makes natural selection succeed as a solution to the problem of improbability, where chance and design both fail at the starting gate? The answer is that natural selection is a cumulative process, which breaks the problem of improbability up into small pieces. Each of the small pieces is slightly improbable, but not prohibitively so.

"He uses a mountain as an example:

The absurd notion that such complexity could spontaneously self-assemble is symbolized by leaping from the foot of the cliff to the top in one bound. Evolution, by contrast, goes around the back of the mountain and creeps up the gentle slope to the summit; easy! The principle of climbing the gentle slope as opposed to leaping up the precipice is so simple, one is tempted to marvel that it took so long for a Darwin to arrive on the scene and discover it.[29]

"So if you agree with the idea of natural selection, you must not agree with Richard Dawkin's view of natural selection?" I asked.

Ken replied, "You're right. To claim that natural selection results in the kind of new information that is needed for molecules-to-man evolution is giving it credit for what it cannot do."

NATURAL SELECTION CLARIFIED

• • •

"I'd like to invite one of my colleagues in to discuss this further," Ken replied. "Her name is Dr. Georgia Purdom. She has a PhD in molecular genetics from Ohio State University, and she has published on this very subject. So if it's all right with you, let's consult an expert."

With that ringing endorsement, Ken picked up the phone, called Dr. Purdom, whose office was right down the hall, and within a few minutes she was seated with us in Ken's office, ready to discuss natural selection.

"People confuse natural selection and evolution all the time," she began in her kind, soft voice. "If it is discovered that mice have a coat color change, or bacteria develops antibiotic resistance, people call this evolution in action, when it is more precisely a good example of natural selection."

"Why the confusion?" I asked.

"Because people like Richard Dawkins see natural selection as the primary

It's a boy.

mechanism that drives evolution. But with molecules-to-man evolution you are giving natural selection a power that it does not have—the power to add new information to the genome, which molecules-to-man evolution requires. But natural selection cannot do that, because it works with information that already exists."

"So there is no gain of information in the process of natural selection?" I asked.

"That's right," Dr. Purdom answered while Ken nodded and smiled broadly from behind his desk.

"Let's look at an example," she offered graciously. "Let's talk about dogs—specifically the length of their fur. It will illustrate the possibilities and limitations of natural selection. Actually I contributed an entire chapter to one of Ken's books where I discuss the whole subject of natural selection and I use dogs as an example."

Right on cue, Ken handed the book to Dr. Purdom. She quickly found the chapter to which she referred and read out loud:

> There are many different dog species—some with long fur and some with short fur. The original dog kind, most likely resembling today's wolf, had several variants of the gene for fur length. L will be the variant of the gene representing long fur and S will be the variant representing short fur.
>
> The original dog kind most likely would have been a mixture of the genes specifying fur length, including both L and S. Because of this makeup, they also most likely had the characteristics of medium fur length. When the original kind [LS dogs] mated, their genetic variability could be seen in their offspring in three ways—LL for long fur, LS for medium fur, and SS for short fur.
>
> If two long fur dogs then mated, the only possible outcome for the offspring is LL, long fur. As can be seen in the example that follows, the long fur dogs have lost the S gene variant and are thus not capable of producing dogs with short fur or medium fur. This loss may be an advantage if those long fur dogs live in an area with cold temperatures. The long fur dogs would then be naturally selected for, as they would

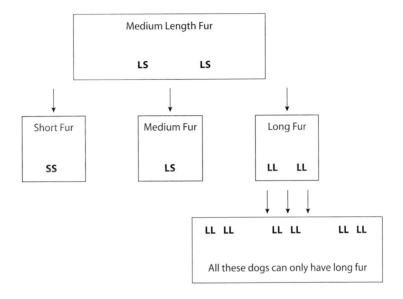

survive better in the given environment. Eventually the majority of this area's dog population would have long fur.

However, the loss of the S variant could be a disadvantage to the long fur dogs if the climate became warmer or if the dogs moved to a warmer climate. Because of the decreased genetic variety [no S gene], they would be unable to produce dogs with short fur, which would be needed to survive better in a warm environment. In this situation, the long fur dogs would be naturally selected against and die....

It can be seen that:

1. Through natural selection, genetic information [variety] was lost.
2. The long fur dogs survive better in a cold environment; they are less able to survive in a warm environment and vice versa.
3. A particular characteristic in the dog population was selected for.
4. Dogs are still dogs since the variation is within the boundaries of 'kind.'

Natural selection of designed variation within the dog kind is not an example of evolution because it does not lead to the formation of a different kind of animal such as a horse, bear, or human. Instead, it is evidence of God's grace in supplying for His creation in the altered environments of a post-Fall, post-Flood world.[30]

"From a creationist perspective," Dr. Purdom said, "natural selection is a process whereby organisms possessing specific characteristics (reflective of their genetic makeup) survive better than others in a given environment or under a given selective pressure (like antibiotic resistance in bacteria). Those with certain characteristics live and those without them diminish in number or die.

"The problem for evolutionists is that natural selection is nondirectional—meaning should the environment change or the selective process be removed, those organisms with previously selected characteristics are typically less able to deal with the changes and may be selected against because their genetic information has decreased."

"So in Richard Dawkins's mountain example," I asked, "the loss of information would actually be a small step down, not up?"

"Exactly."

"If natural selection has never shown the ability to increase information in the DNA, but rather the loss of information, how can an Oxford professor argue for it to be the means of evolution?"

"You would have to ask him!" she responded with a grin.

Ken smiled as well and rejoined the conversation. "Dr. Purdom, while you're reading from your chapter, would you share with Steve what you wrote about speciation?" He turned to me and said, "This topic will interest you as well. We also accept speciation as part of God's plan. But it's all in how you define it."

SPECIATION
· · ·

Dr. Purdom graciously explained, "We see speciation as a possible outcome of natural selection. Here's what I wrote:

IT'S ESTIMATED AMERICANS SPEND 30 BILLION A YEAR ON PROGRAMS, TREATMENTS, SEMINARS AND A MULTITUDE OF OTHER THINGS TO FIND PEACE, HOPE AND CONTENTMENT.

✦

WE'D RECOMMEND SPENDING A LITTLE TIME EACH DAY.

These are the words that can make you wise when you follow them. Guide you through life's troubled waters. And bring a lasting joy to your heart.* And the nice thing is, you don't have to go away on vacation, attend a seminar, or get on a treadmill. All you have to do is open your heart...and start reading. *paraphrased from Psalm 19

A species can be defined as a population of organisms produced by a parent population that has changed so significantly that it can no longer interbreed with the parent population. Using the example of dogs, it is possible that long fur dogs might change sufficiently (other changes besides fur might also be selected for living in cold environments) to the point that they can no longer mate with short fur or medium fur dogs.

Although evolutionists claim that speciation takes long periods of time (millions of years), they are often amazed at how fast species can be observed to form today. Speciation has been observed to occur in as little as a few years, as seen in guppies, lizards, fruit flies, mosquitoes, finches, and mice. This observation does not come as a surprise to creationists as all species alive in the past and today would have had to be produced in fewer than 6,000 years from the original created kinds. In fact, such processes (and perhaps other genetic factors) would have occurred rapidly after the Flood, producing variation within each kind. Such effects are largely responsible for generating the tremendous diversity seen in the living world.

Speciation has never been observed to form an organism of a different kind, such as a dog species producing a cat. Speciation works only within a kind. Evolution requires natural selection and speciation to give rise to new kinds from a former kind (e.g. dinosaurs evolving into birds). Speciation, however, leads to a loss of information, not the gain of information required by evolution. Thus, speciation, as a possible outcome of natural selection cannot be used as a mechanism for 'molecules to man' evolution.[31]

"Steve, as you can see, we agree with the evolutionists on natural selection and speciation, but it's just that we define the terms differently," Ken concluded.

"All this information has been so helpful," I offered as I glanced down at my watch and realized our time was quickly coming to a close.

I thanked Ken and Georgia for their time and valuable insights and made my way to the rental car for my return flight back home to Oklahoma City. The biblical worldview was making more and more sense. We really are "God breathed." We have a conscience. We have an ability to make moral decisions. Therefore, we have value unlike the animal or plant kingdom.

On the plane back from Cincinnati, I realized how privileged I was to spend the time I did with John Stonestreet, David Barton, and Ken Ham—all experts in their chosen fields of study. It provided some important information and documentation regarding how and why the biblical worldview really is absolute and absolutely from God.

Looking out over the clouds from the window of the plane, my mind wandered to the next level in our discussion. Why should we trust that the Bible is God's Word? Why should we believe that Jesus is the Son of God, as He claimed to be? Who can underscore and affirm the evidence for a case for Christ? I knew exactly who I wanted to talk to next. I made a note to ask my secretary to make all the necessary preparations for another trip. I have someone I need to talk with in Denver, Colorado. •

Born that man no more may die...

...For to us a child is born, to us a son is given, and the government will be on his shoulders. And he will be called Wonderful Counselor, Mighty God, Everlasting Father, Prince of Peace. Isaiah 9:6 NIV

7

THE TRUTH OF THE BIBLE

Now that we have a better understanding of the fact that all of us have a worldview, that our forefathers structured our form of government around a biblical worldview, and that the evidence points to an intelligent designer, it is time to turn our attention to another important question: If we are going to base our view of life on the teachings of the Bible, how can we be certain that the Bible is true? It claims to be the Word of God. It teaches that Jesus Christ is the very Son of God. How can we know that these claims are not false? Is there any evidence to help us in our quest?

I knew who I wanted to interview in order to get the answers I needed to these questions.

It was a beautiful Colorado morning when I pulled my rental car into the driveway of a lovely home in a suburb of Denver. I rang the doorbell by the front door and was warmly welcomed by Lee Strobel and his wife, Leslie. A handsome couple, Lee looks to be in his fifties, dressed very stylishly in an all-black ensemble, and he impressed me immediately with his contagious zest for life. Leslie, petite, engaging and with a warm smile, ushered me into their spacious family room, where couches surrounded an oversized coffee table. On the coffee table was a large tray filled with carafes of coffee, tea, and cold water. Lee poured us both a tall glass of water, and I settled into a cozy spot on one of the couches, unaware that I wouldn't be moving for several hours because I was about to be mesmerized by a man who really knows what he's talking about.

Lee Strobel's personal story is a testimony to the supremacy of the biblical worldview. Born and raised in greater Chicago, he graduated from the University of Missouri with an undergraduate degree in journalism. From there he received his master of studies in law degree from Yale Law School. He went to work for the *Chicago Tribune,* where he eventually rose up the ranks to become their legal editor. During all those early years he was a self-proclaimed atheist, thoroughly skeptical of the claims of Christ.

But something happened in 1981. Lee's wife, Leslie, had become a Christian two years earlier, and she immediately began praying for Lee to do the same. Lee didn't do anything halfway, so rather than ignorantly accept it or reject it, he set out to examine the claims of Christ in the way a lawyer or investigative reporter would set out to prove or disprove a case they were working. The result was life-changing for Lee. He accepted the Lord Jesus as his personal savior in 1981 and has been an earnest defender of the faith ever since. His book *The Case for Christ* has sold millions of copies and has helped scores of people better understand the truth about Jesus. If anyone would be able to help me understand the reliability of the Scriptures, it would certainly be this man, with his wealth of knowledge springing from his personal study of the same issues.

"So, Lee, tell me why you would consider the New Testament a reliable source in teaching us about Jesus," I began.

"Steve, I've thought a great deal in preparation for this interview." His booming voice punctuated every word. "What I want to present to you is what a lawyer would call a *cumulative case.* The easiest way to understand it is that, in a cumulative case, one builds the argument piece by piece, brick by brick. Maybe you wouldn't see the individual bricks as all that important by themselves, but each brick is significant in creating the entire building."

"I see what you're saying," I said.

"It's important to understand that when I began to investigate the Bible, I did so as a skeptic. I was an atheist since my teenage years, and it was my wife's conversion to Christianity and the positive changes in her character and values that encouraged me to systematically investigate if there was any credibility to Christianity or any other world religion. I used my legal training and my journalism training to pursue that for approximately two years. In the course of doing so, I did not consider the Bible to be anything special. I didn't consider it to be the Word of God. I didn't consider it to be inerrant or inspired or special in any way. I only considered it to be what it undeniably is, which is a set of ancient historical documents.

"I knew that you could take any ancient document, like the writings of Tacitus or Josephus, and probe those writings to try to ascertain whether or not they're telling you the truth about what they're reporting on. You can take those same techniques and apply them to the Bible. What I didn't do was open the Bible, and when it says it's 'God-breathed' or the 'Word of God,' automatically believe it. I was more skeptical than that. Perhaps you will have readers who themselves are asking questions like 'How can I trust the Bible? Should I trust the Bible? Is the Bible reliable? Does it tell me something true about what God has done in history?'"

I nodded, knowing that may be the exact description of some who read these words.

"There have been many, many skeptics who have investigated the Bible," Lee continued. "A famous example is Sir William Ramsey. He was the son of atheists and himself was an atheist. He grew up in England, a PhD, a noted archaeologist, who believed that the Bible was inaccurate and could be proven so because of archaeology. He moved to the Turkey, spending his lifetime doing archaeological digs. After doing that, he walked away saying that Luke (who is responsible for approximately a quarter of the New Testament, having written the Gospel of Luke and the book of Acts) should be ranked among the greatest historians ever—because archaeology kept confirming over and over and over again what he had written. Imagine that—an atheist who found confirmation of the Bible through archaeology!

"Another example is Sir Lionel Luckhoo, the most successful lawyer who ever lived, according to *The Guinness Book of World's Records*. He is listed as having two hundred forty-five consecutive murder acquittals, either before the jury or on appeal! He was a skeptic concerning the resurrection of Jesus, so he took his monumental legal skills and applied them to the historical record. His conclusion, I can recite to you in one sentence: 'I say unequivocally that the evidence for the resurrection of Jesus Christ is so overwhelming that it compels acceptance by proof which leaves absolutely no room for doubt.'

"So in the time we have together this morning, I'd like us to consider seven bricks that are all put together to form a cumulative case for the reliability of Jesus and the New Testament." He took a long drink of water, signaling me that I was about to hear a defense for the faith that would blow me away.

"Let me have it, Lee!" I encouraged. "Give it to me, brick by brick."

EARLY AND EYEWITNESS-BASED ACCOUNTS
· · ·

"First of all, we have the early and eyewitness nature of the New Testament accounts. Think about the writers of the four Gospels. Remember, Steve, all four of those Gospels were originally anonymous—that is, there were no names attached to them. But the uniform testimony of the early church, along with the explicit testimony of Papias in about 125 AD and Irenaeus in about 180 AD, confirms what the early church had accepted from the beginning: Matthew was a disciple of Jesus, a hated tax collector who became a follower of Christ. Mark essentially was the interpreter for Peter, so he was giving Peter's account of what had taken place. John was a disciple, actually one of the inner circle—therefore another eyewitness. And Luke was a first-century investigative reporter as well as a companion of Paul, who was an eyewitness to the resurrected Jesus. These four Gospel authors were not just contemporaries—they were either personally eyewitnesses or they were reporting the accounts of eyewitnesses!

"The apostle Peter put it this way: 'We did not follow cleverly invented stories when we told you about the power and coming of our Lord Jesus Christ, but we were eyewitnesses of his majesty.' [2 Peter 1:16]

"The Apostle John wrote these words: 'That which was from the beginning, which we have heard, which we have seen with our eyes, which we have looked at and our hands have touched—this we proclaim concerning the Word of Life.' [1 John 1:1]

"Luke, the investigative reporter, said: 'Many have undertaken to draw up an account of the things that have been fulfilled among us, just as they were handed down to us by those who from the first were eyewitnesses and servants of the word. Therefore, since I myself have carefully investigated everything from the beginning, it seemed good also to me to write an orderly account for you, most excellent Theophilus.' [Luke 1:1–3]

"By the way," Lee interjected. "If you made up the four Gospel writers, certainly you would have used James or Peter rather than Matthew and Mark! Matthew was a tax collector—a hated profession. Why add controversy to the picture by including the writings of a notoriously hated man? And why use Mark? He wasn't even a disciple, just a person who got the account from Peter. Why would you make it up that way? Stick with the disciples themselves!

"Another part of this argument to consider is the fact that the first century was a time one could characterize as an oral culture. In other words, people could memorize vast portions of writings or things that had been said. Remember, there were no tape recorders at that time," he added, pointing to the small tape recorder I was using to preserve this interview and aid in the writing of this chapter. "So there was some oral preservation that took place, and that was not uncommon for the times."

Lee stopped for a sip of water, and then took up where he left off. "Even most liberal scholars date the writing of Mark's Gospel in the 70s, Matthew and Luke in the 80s, and John in the 90s. My point is that even with this later dating of the books, they were still written down during the lifetimes of Jesus' contemporaries. So if they were exaggerating or making stuff up, people could have refuted it based on their own knowledge of what had taken place. In fact, we see just the opposite. In Acts 2 we read of over three thousand people choosing to follow Christ after Peter's inspiring, Spirit-filled message. Part of what he did was appeal to their common knowledge:

> Men of Israel, listen to this; Jesus of Nazareth was a man accredited by God to you by miracles, wonders and signs, which God did **among you** through him, **as you yourselves** know....
>
> God has raised this Jesus to life, and **we are all witnesses** of the fact. (Acts 2:22, 32, emphasis added)

"Do you agree with these late dates for the writing of the Gospels?" I asked.

"I'm glad you asked that question, Steve, because I believe Luke helps us see that those dates for the Gospels are much later than they should be. Luke wrote Luke and Acts as a two-part work," Lee responded immediately, as if he knew I would raise the question. "Acts ends with Paul's house arrest. It doesn't talk about Paul's death. It doesn't talk about James's death. It doesn't talk about the Jewish-Roman War. It doesn't talk about the destruction of the temple. All of these things occurred between the early 60s and 70 AD. Why aren't these things mentioned in Acts? Because they probably occurred after the book of Acts was written. Therefore, I think you can date Acts to around 60 AD. Since Acts is part two of a two-part work, we can conclude that Luke was written *before* 60 AD."

"Interesting," I said.

"Yes, it is," he replied. "We know that Matthew and Luke took some of their material from Mark, so Mark had to be written earlier. Paul's writings are even earlier than Mark."

Lee got very, very intense at this point, so I knew we were in for a strong statement. "Here's the most intriguing thing of all: Paul's writings start in the late 40s and 50s AD. But he embeds in his writings pieces of creeds and hymns of the earliest church. These hymns and creeds go back even earlier yet, because he's already embedded them in his writings. He's producing the earliest writings, but he's quoting earlier stuff still! And that stuff tends to affirm things like the deity of Jesus and His resurrection. Philippians 2 talks about Jesus being "in very nature God.""

You're to die for.

Colossians 1 speaks of Jesus being "the image of the invisible God." These are parts of early hymns and creeds that date back to the dawning of the Christian faith."

The intensity was rising. "But the most important one is in First Corinthians 15, starting at verse 3. This is the report of a creed of the earliest church that summarizes the resurrection of Jesus. Most scholars will tell you that Jesus was crucified in 30 or 33 AD. Paul had been Saul of Tarsus, a man commissioned to arrest, try, and see Christians executed for their heresy. He was converted about two years after Jesus' death, when he encounters the resurrected Christ on the road to Damascus. Three years after that, Paul goes to Jerusalem and meets personally with James and Peter. Many scholars will tell you that it was at this meeting that Paul was most likely given this creed by these two individuals—both of whom are specifically mentioned in the creed!

"This creed contains the essence of Christianity. It says Jesus died—why? For our sins. He was buried. On the third day He was resurrected from the dead. And then it mentions specific names of eyewitnesses, including skeptics, whose lives were changed one hundred eighty degrees because they encountered the resurrected Jesus.

"If Paul were given this creed within five years of Jesus' life on earth, the creed was already in creedal form by then, prior to that. Therefore, this material goes right back to the beginning! One of the most famous New Testament scholars, James D. G. Dunn, said it this way: 'This tradition [the First Corinthians 15 creed] we can be entirely certain was formulated as tradition within months of Jesus' life.'

"Here's why that's important," Lee continued. "As a skeptic, I used to think the divinity of Jesus, proven by His resurrection from the dead, was a later legend. It takes a long time for a legend to develop, and I thought this one would've taken maybe a couple of hundred years. But here we have a news flash that goes right back to the beginning, that tells us the earliest beliefs of the church happened to deal with the divinity of Jesus and His resurrection from the dead. There was no time for legend to develop. It would be unprecedented in the history of the world for a legend to develop that fast and wipe out a solid core of historical truth!

"Based on this and all the various evidence that I detail in my books, I think the conclusion is clear: Jesus claimed to be the Son of God and convincingly authenticated that claim by rising from the dead."

THE CRITERION OF EMBARRASSMENT
· · ·

"It sounds like it's time for another brick in our cumulative case," I offered, anxious and curious to see where we would be going next.

"Second, we have what is referred to as the criterion of embarrassment."

"The criterion of embarrassment?" I asked. "That's a new phrase for me. Exactly what does that mean?"

"In its simplest form, it means that if you were making all this stuff up, you would never include things that would potentially embarrass you. On the contrary, you would make yourself look good."

"Can you give me an example or two of what you're talking about?"

"Sure." He paused, took another sip of water, and settled back into the comfortable couch. "Who found the stone rolled away at the empty tomb on Easter morning? Women, right?"

"Correct," I nodded.

"Women? In first-century Jewish and Roman culture, the testimony of women was not generally considered to be credible. Generally, they were not even allowed to testify in a court of law and were thought to be unreliable. So it's embarrassing that women discovered the tomb empty. If the Gospel writers were merely inventing the story out of thin air, they would never have claimed women discovered the tomb. That would hurt their case! They would have said John or Peter—any man—discovered it empty.

"But the very fact that they did report women discovered the empty tomb tells me that they are telling the truth. They were apparently so concerned to be accurate in their reporting that they included this fact even though it was embarrassing to them and weakened their case in front of the first-century audience they were trying to convince.

"You see these sorts of things all throughout the New Testament. Another example is the disciples—half the time they seem to come off as knuckleheads," Lee continued with a wry smile. "They don't understand what Jesus is saying. Peter denied Christ three times. How humiliating is that? Why in the world would you make one of the leaders of the church look so foolish if you were making up the stuff?! This suggests to me that the Gospel writers were committed to reporting what actually occurred, even if it made the disciples look bad."

"Is there an example in history of a writer who would stretch the truth that would serve as a contrast to what you're saying?" I interjected.

Lee paused for a moment, deep in thought. His eyes widened as he realized an excellent example. "Consider the first-century Jewish historian Josephus. Everyone knew he was working for the Romans. So there are times in his writings where he tends to skew things in order to make the Romans look a little better than they really were. Scholars know that about him, so they tend to compensate for his bias."

"Josephus is seeing things through rose-colored glasses," I mumbled.

"Exactly," Lee confirmed. "But I believe the four Gospel writers, even though they were making the case for Jesus as the Son of God, were committed to reporting what actually took place—and they just let the chips fall where they may. That's what the criterion of embarrassment suggests to us."

ARCHAEOLOGICAL CONFIRMATION
· · ·

"How else can we test the New Testament?" Lee asked. "The third brick in our cumulative case is through archaeology. This brick can't tell us directly that Jesus is the Son of God, but it can help us corroborate some of the *accuracy* of the reports about Him." He leaned forward and brought extra emphasis when he said the word *accuracy*.

"Archaeology can test the incidental details. I'll give you an example. In Luke 3:1 he refers to a man named Lysanias and calls him the tetrarch of Abilene in about 27 AD. For years scholars pointed to this as evidence that Luke didn't know what he was talking about, since everybody knew Lysanias was not a tetrarch but rather the ruler of Chalcis who died half a century earlier. If Luke can't get the basic facts right, they suggested, nothing he has written can be trusted."

"They've got a point," I admitted.

"That's when archaeology stepped in," Lee pressed on. "An inscription was later found from the time of Tiberius, from 14–37 AD, which identifies Lysanias as tetrarch of Abila near Damascus. It was just as Luke had written! It turns out there had been two government officials named Lysanias! Luke was correct after all.

"So here's the point: as a skeptic I had to ask myself the question, if Luke was so careful to get these incidental details correct, why would I think he would be any less credible when he is talking about really important things, like Jesus rising from the dead, thus proving He is the Son of God?"

EXTRABIBLICAL CORROBORATION
• • •

"The next brick we have is the corroboration from sources outside the Bible. What do these extrabiblical writings tell us about the accuracy of the New Testament?

"When I was writing *The Case for Christ,* I interviewed Dr. Edwin Yamauchi of Miami University in Ohio. He is brilliant on the subject of corroborating evidence. I asked him to play pretend with me. I said, 'If we didn't have the New Testament or any other Christian writings, what would we know about Jesus from ancient non-Christian sources, like Josephus, the Talmud, Tacitus, Pliny the Younger, and others? He smiled, letting me know there was quite a bit of information available. He put it this way:

> We would know that, first, Jesus was a Jewish teacher; second, many people believed that He performed healings and exorcisms; third, some people believed He was the Messiah; fourth, He was rejected by the Jewish leaders; fifth, He was crucified under Pontius Pilate in the reign of Tiberius; sixth, despite this shameful death, His followers, who believed He was still alive, spread beyond Palestine so that there were multitudes of them in Rome by AD 64; and seventh, all kinds of people

from the cities and countryside—men and women, slave and free—worshiped Him as God.

"Wouldn't you say that's a pretty impressive outline of the life of Jesus?" Lee smiled as he leaned toward me.

"Yes, it is," I replied. "That's very impressive."

"There is also a fabulous book by Dr. Gary Habermas entitled *The Verdict of History*. In it, he details a list of thirty-nine ancient sources that document the life of Jesus, from which he enumerates over one hundred reported facts concerning Jesus' life, teachings, crucifixion, and resurrection. Twenty-four of the sources, including seven secular sources and several of the earliest creeds of the church, specifically concern the divine nature of Jesus. That's what I would call persuasive corroboration."

"I would agree," I smiled.

"Well, I can continue if you'd like," he smiled warmly.

"By all means, please continue," I urged. I was thoroughly engrossed with his every word. This was all quite wonderful!

MESSIANIC PROPHECY FULFILLMENT
• • •

"The fifth brick is the fulfillment of ancient prophecies from the Old Testament in the New Testament. This is the argument that shows that the Bible is not human but divine in origin. There is no other book like that. It's been estimated that there are one hundred ninety-one prophecies about Jesus in the Old Testament, but most scholars emphasize around forty-eight of them that they consider to be 'major prophecies.'

"Skeptics often argue that many of the prophecies could have been known by Jesus, so He could have intentionally fulfilled them. They usually point to one like the prophecy in Zechariah 9:9 that the Messiah would ride into Jerusalem on a donkey. They say He knew that was written, so He made sure He chose a donkey to ride in order to fool the people into believing He was their Messiah. I get their point.

"But there are so many prophecies that are beyond what Jesus could have prearranged. His method of birth, His method of death, His lineage, the fact that not a bone of His body would be broken during His execution, which was not at all in keeping with how the Romans generally practiced crucifixion. They frequently broke a person's legs so he could no longer push up on the cross in order to lessen the stress on his chest muscles in order to keep breathing. But not Jesus. He could not have arranged these things in advance.

"A scientist attempted to estimate the odds of any person throughout history fulfilling these forty-eight prophecies. The result? The chances were one in one trillion, trillion, trillion, trillion, trillion, trillion, trillion, trillion, trillion, trillion, trillion, trillion, trillion.

"So this tells me something that I find extremely important and powerful." He paused long enough for me to lean toward him so I wouldn't miss a word.

"The Bible is not only true. It's divine."

THE TRANSMISSION OF THE TEXT THROUGH TIME

• • •

"The sixth brick is the transmission of the biblical text through time. We don't have the original writings preserved for us, but we do have a wealth of manuscript evidence. Remember, Steve, until the invention of the printing press, the whole Bible had to be copied by hand. That's important, because that means that in the writing of the text over and over and over, there have to be some minor mistakes.

"A professor gave me this illustration. Take a high school social studies class and ask them to write out by hand the Declaration of Independence. The A students would complete the project without very many mistakes. The B students would make a few more mistakes. The C students even more, and so on down the line to the F students. But by comparing and contrasting the various copies, we could pretty easily get back to the original wording of the Declaration. Similarly, with the New Testament, we have so many manuscripts that we can confidently get back to what the originals said in virtually every instance simply by comparing them one with another."

"Approximately how many manuscripts do we have?" I asked.

"At last count, there are around twenty-five thousand handwritten manuscripts of the New Testament in the various ancient languages," he replied with zest. "Just as a point of comparison, we have around six hundred copies of the second best preserved ancient text, Homer's *Iliad*. Plus, there are over *one million* quotations from the Bible in the writings of the early church fathers.

"Now, let's be fair. Are there some controversies? Yes. Experts say there are between two hundred thousand and four hundred thousand variants in the ancient manuscripts, but let's also be clear—eighty percent of those variants are things like minor spelling errors that don't even get translated into English. Only two percent of the variants affect the meaning of the text to some degree and have a decent chance of going back to the original text. But here's the key point: not one church doctrine is in any way jeopardized."

"Give me an example of a place where scholars are not one hundred percent sure of the original," I prodded.

"Sure. In Romans 5:1, some manuscripts say, "we have peace" while other manuscripts say, "let us have peace." There's only one character in the Greek that changes it. So what? That's not a big controversy! It doesn't make any difference, really! My point is that it doesn't affect any belief. Besides, good Bibles footnote these issues so readers will be aware of them."

PERSONAL AFFIRMATION

• • •

"The seventh and final brick is what I call the personal evidence. When I was an atheist, I read the teachings of Jesus. I saw an incredible beauty and moral strength in His teachings. I applied His words to my life and made a discovery—they work! Forgive others? That concept alone was thoroughly against my nature, but as we all know, it is good for me to be a forgiving person.

"When you apply the teachings of Jesus, they change you. I remember going to church with Leslie while I was still a skeptic and hearing the biblical teachings on marriage. We came home and began to apply what we had learned, and it began improving my marriage from the outset.

"So it got me thinking about all I was learning. I remember musing over the idea 'it must come from a source beyond human reasoning.' Here I was, living the life of a hard-drinking, narcissistic, self-centered man, but by investigating the evidence, the only way I could maintain my atheism was to swim upstream against the river of evidence. My training in the law and journalism led me to find the truth. And when I say I did investigation, I did it for all the major religions. The others didn't even come close. The credentials of the Bible are unique. If it is reliable and it passes the tests, then I had to ask myself the question, What does it say to me?

"I read John 1:12: 'Yet to all who received him, to those who believed in his name, he gave the right to become children of God.'

"I realized that, based on the evidence of history, I intellectually believed Jesus is the unique Son of God, but I needed to receive Him as my Savior. And that's exactly what I did on November 8, 1981. And that one decision not only affected me, but it affected the entire Strobel family."

"And millions of other people," I silently thought to myself. "The power of the Gospel taught in the Word of God."

As our time drew to a close, I thanked Lee profusely for all the hard work and extra effort he had put into this interview. Since he has written many books with this same interview style, it was obvious to me that he had gone the extra mile to make our time together profitable. I drove back to the Denver airport excited about the seven bricks I had learned that put together this cumulative case.

The foundation for relying on God's Word was in place. But I couldn't help but replay the final brick in my mind—the personal effect God and His Word have on people. A few hours later, as I sat on the plane, almost in a daze, my mind was flooded with so many stories of people who have been impacted by true Christianity in practice. Individuals, neighborhoods, cultures, and nations—the entrance of a biblical worldview changes lives. In the next chapter, I'd like to share some of those stories with you. •

WHAT ARE YOU FOLLOWING?

"Where is He who has been born King of the Jews?
For we have seen His star in the East and have come to worship Him."
Matthew 2:2

8

THE BIBLICAL WORLDVIEW IN PRACTICE

Now that we have discussed in some detail the reasons behind accepting the biblical worldview, let's look at the difference it makes in people's lives. Does the biblical worldview impact those who believe it and those who are exposed to it? The answer is an emphatic *yes!* The following accounts are dramatic indeed, and they help us understand the power of the Gospel of Jesus Christ.

KAMAL SALEEM

• • •

In the heart of the Middle East, a boy was born into a large Sunni Muslim family in 1957. His parents named him Kamal Saleem.[32] He lived with his mother and father and fourteen brothers and sisters in a three-room house. "Islam defined everything in my life," Kamal recalls. "We bowed to Allah five times a day, and every aspect of life was built around him."

At an early age Kamal was pulled out of school by his father so he could go to work and help support the family. He remembers an incident when he was on his way home from work with his day's wage and he was attacked and robbed by some older boys. The pain of the fight paled in comparison to his father's harsh words when Kamal returned home empty-handed. "I wish you were a girl," his father lamented. "I'd have given you away by now."

"I hated home," Kamal confesses, "so work was pleasurable."

Getting beat up became a regular routine for Kamal. One day he nursed his wounds by ducking into a mosque. "You have to become a man," he was told. "You have to become strong." The group of men at the mosque took him in, befriended him, cared for him, and protected him. The group was called the Muslim Brotherhood, a fundamentalist extremist organization.

By the way, here's an important tidbit of information to consider: these events began when Kamal was only *seven years old!*

This new found 'brotherhood' took him to Assault Camp, where he learned to shoot an AK-47 assault rifle. At the tender age of seven, his gun shaking in his small hands and shooting wildly, it was a transforming experience for the youngster. "I thought I was James Bond," he remembers. "My ultimate goal was to serve Allah with all I had. I felt empowered. I felt that I was chosen."

By the time he was a young teenager, he began to be recruited by all manner of terrorist organizations. Ultimately, Kamal joined the Palestine Liberation Organization (PLO) in order to make steady attacks on Israel and other enemies of Allah. Christians and Jews are considered infidels by the fundamentalists, and if they did not convert to Islam, the only other option was that they were to be systematically destroyed.

The first time his group attacked Israel, they considered it a success. The second mission was not so fortunate. They were ambushed. Kamal remembers his good friend being shot while standing right next to him. Kamal picked him up, draped him over his shoulders, and retreated. By the time they made it to safety, his friend was dead, not because of the original wound, but from the multiple wounds he received while on Kamal's shoulders. His friend's body served as a human shield, protecting Kamal from enemy fire. Kamal felt great sadness about his friend, but he also perceived it as Allah's special protection over him. "Once again, I felt chosen," he said.

It was at this time that Kamal was working on his ultimate goal—to get to the United States. He wanted to convert as many American Christians and Jews to "the glory of Allah" and destroy the rest. After all, the United States was viewed as the "Great Satan" by Muslim fundamentalists.

Kamal was successful in making his way to America. Kamal had been studying the language and the culture, for many years as a part of fulfilling Islam's *altaqiyah* teaching, which a part of is the strategy to "blend in with the enemy." Life was going along according to plan until 1985, when Kamal's world changed forever.

While driving his car one afternoon, another car suddenly swerved into his lane, forcing Kamal to move out of the lane to avoid hitting it. But moving out of that lane put him into a position where a truck, which seemingly came out of nowhere, broadsided him, sending the car crashing off the road. Kamal was thrown from his vehicle, ending up face down in the mud off to the side.

"Where are you, Allah?" Kamal recalls crying out. But no answer was to be heard. A stranger appeared and began attending to his needs. An ambulance was called, and the man waited with Kamal. The man cleaned him up with his shirt and used his body to block the sun from Kamal's eyes. The man smiled at Kamal and said, "Don't worry. Everything is going to be all right."

The ambulance arrived, and Kamal was taken to the local hospital. His left side was in pretty bad shape, as he had two fractured vertebrae in his neck and other injuries, so an orthopedic surgeon was brought in. "We will take care of you," the doctor promised, and he did. As part of Kamal's rehabilitation, a physical therapist was required and he, too, smiled and offered Kamal nothing but love and reassurance.

These three men—the man who found Kamal in the mud hole, the orthopedic surgeon, and the physical therapist—were all Christians. They took Kamal in as one of their own, and even paid for many of his expenses and a new vehicle.

The impact of three Christians who actually practiced their faith was mind-boggling to Kamal. Living out their biblical worldview was a look at "a loving religion," to use Kamal's words.

"A monster had me," Kamal said. "And the monster was *love*."

In desperation, Kamal began crying out to Allah. "Why did you do this to me, Allah?" he asked. He received no answer. "Speak to me, Allah! Let me know that you are real." He heard absolutely nothing. By now Kamal was utterly despondent, and as a result, he grabbed his gun, preparing to take his own life. "I know that if I take my own life, Allah will send me to hell," he confessed. "But I concluded it was better to live in hell then with Allah, because he would not speak to me."

"That's when it hit me," he recalls. "I suddenly thought, *'Give the God of Father Abraham a chance.'* And that's what I did."

He further remembers, "I fell to my knees and said, 'God of Father Abraham, speak to me.'"

The Lord did speak to Kamal and said, "Arise, my son, and be an ambassador of Mine!"

"I heard the birds singing," Kamal recalls. "I saw the wind blowing in the trees. I thought of the love and the kindness of my three new friends. I got off my knees...and miraculously my left side was healed! I felt like Pinocchio had become a real boy. My world was completely changed!"

Kamal began to study the Bible. Little by little, he began to sever his life from his past. It was the hardest thing he had ever done, because he had become so entrenched in the Muslim world, but he knew it was the only thing to do.

Today, Kamal Saleem has a new goal—to bring Muslims to Christ. "I want them to see the Father who loves them and wants them to come home." According to his ministry Web site, www.koomeministries.com, "Kamal and his wife, Victoria, have three children and five grandchildren. Eight years ago his local church ordained Kamal as a minister of the Gospel of Jesus Christ. He currently teaches and speaks worldwide in churches, Jewish synagogues, Muslim communities, law enforcement organizations, universities, high schools, and to political leaders. Kamal carries a message from God to awaken the church through the truth, education, and relationships, and to pray for our enemies with unconditional love."

In a very important distinction, Kamal concludes, "*Allah in not a god of relationships.*" But he adds, "Those three men who found me and loved me unconditionally, they were the ones God used to help me step into the light."

The story of Kamal Saleem is the story of how the biblical worldview, the Gospel of Jesus Christ, is powerful, and it can make a difference in the life of an individual. But God can also work in many individuals, one by one, until He has impacted an entire society. And that is our next example.

THE WAODANI TRIBE OF SOUTH AMERICA
• • •

In the mid-1950s, when Christian missionaries first reached out to the Waodani tribe deep in the heart of eastern Ecuador, sociologists accurately calculated that six out of every ten deaths in this culture were *homicides,* giving them the gruesome distinction of being the most violent society on earth. Many people knew of this tribe as the Aucas, but the name the tribe members called themselves was Waodani.

The Waodani were obsessed with defending their territory. There were accounts of their murdering trespassers as early as the turn of the twentieth century. When oil was discovered on their land, in addition to the value found in their rubber plants, a constant war erupted with outsiders. Stated in the simplest terms, they killed the oil people and the oil people killed them. Anyone who encroached on their land was in danger. Using their most basic weapons, the Waodani clubbed, stabbed, speared, or macheted their victims.

But the Waodani didn't just murder outsiders, they murdered their own as well. Attempts were made through the years to befriend the tribe with gifts, but none were ever effective.

Enter a team of brave American missionaries. Jim and Elisabeth Elliot, Nate and Marj Saint, Nate's sister Rachel, Roger and Barbara Youderian, Ed and Marilou McCully, and Pete and Olive Fleming joined forces for this all-important mission. They all arrived at various times between 1949 and 1955, paving the way for their amazing story that unfolded in the autumn of 1955 and early 1956.

In September 1955 the missionaries began flying over the Waodani long-houses in an attempt to initiate contact. Through a creative invention of Nate's, they were able to extend a rope from the plane with a bucket at the end; it was filled with a variety of simple gifts for the tribe. The Waodani cautiously accepted the gifts, and when the flights continued, they expressed an eagerness for the plane to land. The missionaries spoke to them in simple phrases from the Waodani's native language through a loudspeaker attached to the plane. By November, not only was the tribe freely accepting the gifts from the missionaries, but they were actually returning the kindness by tying little trinkets to the rope after removing what had been dropped for them!

The missionaries viewed this gesture as very positive, so they began looking for a way to contact with the tribe. Nate found a stretch of beach nearby that would be sufficient for landing the aircraft, placing it less than five miles from the center of the tribal community. He named it Palm Beach.

On January 3, 1956, the small plane made several trips to Palm Beach to establish a camp for the five men. Once the men were set up, they flew around the Waodani, announcing over the loudspeaker that they had arrived and inviting the tribe to visit them at their new camp. It took three days for a response, but on January 6 the camp welcomed three Waodani visitors: two women and a man. It all started off well. The missionaries gave their guests gifts, and conversations ensued that took up several hours. Nate noticed the man, whom they nicknamed George, seemed very curious about their airplane, so he took the young man up for a ride! In their tribal language, they referred to the plane as the "wood bee," and soon they were buzzing over the rest of the tribe.

When they landed the plane back at Palm Beach, the young woman, whom they nicknamed Delilah, was growing restless and wanted to return home. George and Delilah left Palm Beach late that afternoon, but the older woman remained and talked through most of the night. It all appeared so encouraging to the five missionaries.

What the five men didn't know was that several men in the Waodani tribe—particularly Delilah's brother—were not happy with what had happened with George and Delilah. The brother was furious that the two of them had been out alone. This was not appropriate behavior toward his sister and his anger raged. In an attempt to take the heat off his own misbehavior, George lied to the tribe, telling them that the outsiders had attacked them, and that's why they were separated from the older woman who had accompanied them. A chorus arose in the heart of the jungle: *Kill the foreigners!*

Two days later, on January 8, the five missionaries anticipated meeting another group of friendly Waodani. From his plane above, Nate saw some men heading toward Palm Beach, so he radioed his wife at 12:30 p.m. to share the good news of the potential meeting. He promised to radio her at 4:30 with an update.

The Waodani visited the camp at Palm Beach, but they came to kill the missionaries.

First, they speared Jim Elliot. Then Pete Fleming. Then Nate Saint, Ed McCully, and Roger Youderian. The Waodani threw the five speared bodies, along with all their possessions, into the muddy river. As a final act of violence, they stripped the airplane of its outer fabric, leaving it as a stark metaphor of the deadly destruction that had occurred.

When Marj did not hear from Nate at 4:30, she became concerned but chose to wait until the evening to alert anyone. The next morning, rescue crews were alerted and flew over the area until they found the men's bodies.

For a particularly moving interview, take a look at the documentary DVD titled *Beyond the Gates of Splendor,* where one of the pilots who discovered the bodies recounts how he came upon them.[33] Five decades later, the dear man cannot recount the story without breaking down into sobs several times. He recalled a comment one of the missionaries had made prior to their flight: "The Aucas aren't ready for heaven...and we are." But this is not the end of the story.

Rachel Saint and Elisabeth Elliot remained in Ecuador, right where they had been prior to the men's martyrdom. Rachel had been friends with a young Waodani woman for some time, which explains how the men learned the tribe's language. Rachel's friend was named Dayuma, and she played a very important role in this story.

One day, around noon, two men came to Elisabeth's door and announced, "We have two Auca women at our house. Do you want to see them?" She responded that she did, so they took her down to where the women were waiting. The women struck up a friendship, and Elisabeth invited them to her house. Elisabeth and Rachel discovered that the two women were Dayuma's aunts. The two felt very comfortable with Rachel and Elisabeth, so they stayed with them. Perhaps some healing was beginning.

Dayuma's aunts told their hosts, "When the palm fruit is ripe, we will go home and we want you to come with us."

"Will they spear me like they did my husband?" Elisabeth inquired.

"Of course not!" they replied, putting their arms around her and laughing, "because you are our friend!"

Looking back, it was clear that the Waodani would have killed a man on sight, but a woman might not be attacked. So they decided to return with them.

The Waodani believed in a creator God. Dayuma, in words that they would understand, communicated with them what Rachel had taught her. "God has marked His trail with Carvings. If we follow His Carvings while we are alive, we will live in His House forever when we die." She told them, "God does not want us to spear each other. We should use the spear only to hunt for food." They used these words from God's Carving to explain the Gospel: "Being speared Himself, God's one and only Son did not spear back. He let Himself be killed so the people killing Him would one day live well."

The message of the Gospel slowly penetrated the tribe's heart. Of course, it is particularly powerful to hear the testimonies of some of the men who participated in the killing of the five missionaries. To hear them speak of how Christ has changed their heart and life is nothing less than miraculous. As one of the warriors put it: "We acted badly, badly, until they brought us God's Carvings. Now we walk His trail."

The most violent society on earth is now quite the opposite, due to their acceptance of the biblical worldview.

Who can overlook the unmistakable power of the biblical worldview in its teaching concerning *forgiveness*. All those American missionary families had to embrace Christian forgiveness in order to extend it to their new tribal brothers and sisters.

This incredible story inspired my brother Mart to become the driving force

He is Risen!

You're pardoned.

Come home.

God is . . .
Ready to pardon,
Gracious and merciful,
Slow to anger,
Abundant in kindness.
Nehemiah 9:17

behind the production of the feature film *End of the Spear.* I sat down with him to ask him to recount the movie's beginning.

Mart said, "I remember being in Lancaster, Pennsylvania, and hearing Marj and Nate's son, Steve, speak on this whole experience. Just when I thought it couldn't get any more amazing, Steve invited to the platform *the man who speared his father!* The story of love, redemption, and forgiveness is almost overpowering."

Mart remembers where it went from there. "I knew a guy who had talked about making a movie about Jim Elliot, so I sent him a tape of Steve's presentation. In the meantime, my friend Rob Hoskins challenged me to step up to the plate and do it myself. 'Mart, you've got to get this movie done!' he encouraged me."

"Did you feel up to the task?" I asked.

"Of course not—you know that!" he replied in a typical brotherly manner. "You know that we hadn't even been to movie theaters at that point in our lives!"

"So go on with the story," I encouraged.

"I needed to contact Steve Saint to see if he would be interested in having this story made into a movie."

"You need to get the permission of the Waodani," he said.

"So we flew to Ecuador, got the permission from the tribe, and put together a production company that we called Every Tribe Entertainment. We filmed the movie in Panama, praying and trusting God all the way. I'm humbled to be able to say that God has used this movie in the lives of many people, for which we are very grateful. It was nearly ten years from the time I first heard Steve speak to the release of the film, but it was all worth it, believe me."

When someone comes from a biblical worldview, they see the incredible power of the Gospel of Christ. It can impact an individual. It can impact a whole society. It can even have an impact on an entire nation.

AIDS IN UGANDA

• • •

Nearly forty million people are living with HIV/AIDS according to the 2006 report on global AIDS published by the UNAIDS organization. The Global AIDS

Alliance adds that eight thousand people die from HIV/AIDS each day, and eleven thousand people are newly infected. Half of those eleven thousand are between the ages of fifteen and twenty-four. Nearly 70 percent of all HIV-infected people in the world live and die in sub-Saharan Africa, according to UNICEF. It is projected that by 2015, more infants will die of AIDS in Botswana than are born in Boston and Philadelphia combined.

After my brother Mart had finished working on the movie *The End of the Spear,* he read a book by Dr. Edward C. Green, a medical anthropologist from the Harvard School of Public Health. In the book, Dr. Green (no relation to my family) expounded on a different way to prevent AIDS infection, a way that had been devised in Africa. Mart was fascinated with this topic, and his interest led to the production of a film titled *Miss HIV.*[34]

The film creatively follows the story of two young women, both HIV positive, who are participating in a pageant for women who have HIV. The pageant is held in Botswana, and its purpose is to destigmatize HIV. Botswana is juxtaposed with Uganda, where the HIV statistics were striking in their difference. In 1992, 10 percent of the population of Botswana has HIV. That figure skyrocketed to 24 percent in 2006. In contrast, in 1992, 15 percent of Uganda's population was infected with HIV (one of the highest percentages in the world at that time). But by 2006, that percentage was dramatically reduced to 6 percent, causing one expert to declare, "It is one of the largest reductions of new infections in recorded history." The difference was in how the two countries approached HIV. Botswana had one policy, Uganda had another.

Uganda's program can be summed up with the acronym ABC:

- Abstinence
- Be faithful in your marriage
- If you cannot do A and B, use a condom

Janet Museveni, first lady of Uganda, said: "We had to fight to defeat AIDS or it would defeat us. Our culture really used to promote abstinence from premarital sex. Uganda is our family and we had to spread that message to everybody."

The irony was that the experts from the Western world told the Ugandans that their program was all wrong. Women's rights groups, for example, didn't like the idea of money being used to promote A and B in the Ugandan ABC program. Most of the Westerners emphasized that condoms were the solution to the HIV/AIDS threat. But it wasn't the solution.

"The strategy of Uganda was to make people *afraid* of AIDS," Edward Green observed. "The good news is it's not transmitted easily. You almost have to go out and look for it." Green then pointed to a sobering statistic: "As condoms become more available, infection rates actually rise."

Dr. Norman Hearst, professor of family medicine and epidemiology at the University of California, San Francisco, wholeheartedly agreed. "The problem with condoms comes if we forget about the A and the B in Africa." He likens using condoms alone to the wearing of seat belts to stop drunk-driving accidents. Granted, seat beats can help to lessen the seriousness of the accident, but it's the drunk driver that's the real issue.

Hearst commented on the Ugandan program known as Zero Grazing: "Don't go outside your marriage was come up with by the Ugandans themselves at a time when very few foreign experts were there telling them what to do."

The people of Uganda understood these concepts, not only in principle, but in the priority in which they were delivered. Martin Ssempa, a Ugandan national, added Hearst's comments. "In Uganda, it was capital A, capital B, and small c," he said. "It was mainly getting married people to reduce the number of partners." Without outside intervention, the Ugandans knew this plan would produce results. After all, it was the biblical worldview being put into practice. And it was to have an impact on the entire nation!

First lady Museveni understood that concept quite clearly:

I believe that the churches are the primary organization that has a burden to get the truth to the people. We wanted to mobilize everybody who can speak to our population to tell them about this enemy. We believed the Church would truly do this best because they already had the burden of speaking to our people and telling them the truth.

We need to come together as God's people who believe if we live the right way in this life, we will defeat sexually transmitted diseases for sure.

There was no getting around the fact that Uganda's ABC plan has its roots in the Bible. Norman Hearst weighed in on the controversy: "People accuse the religious right of being willing to let millions of Africans die for their beliefs because they don't want to give them condoms. Well, unfortunately, in a sense, some people on the left are willing to let millions of Africans die because they don't want to say anything that sounds like they're interfering with their sexual freedom."

Not to be deterred, Ugandan president Yoweri Museveni went from town to town with a bullhorn, telling people that if they didn't change, they would die. "I was eventually assisted by the leaders of the churches and the Muslims, community leaders, political leaders and the media," the president said. Before long, they saw the results in the figures quoted at the beginning of this section.

A Ugandan pastor looked back on the success and said, "[We were told] don't bring the church into this mix? Don't bring faith into this mix? You can educate, but I get the *power* from God. Faith gives the *power.*"

Sadly, even after its success, the ABC program has been largely dismantled in Uganda. Now, thanks to the so-called experts from the West (primarily from the United States), the main thrust is on pushing drugs. Isn't it ironic that the United States is telling Africa how to deal with AIDS, especially when one can clearly see that AIDS infections are slowly declining in Africa but on the rise here at home!

How could this situation be happening on our home soil? It's because America is moving away from the biblical worldview on which it was founded. In the next few chapters, let's take a look at the positive side—people who lived out their biblical worldview in our country and the successes they achieved. Then we will look at an example of how we have lost our way. •

"It is the duty of all nations to acknowledge the providence of Almighty God, to obey His will, to be grateful for His benefits, and humbly to implore His protection and favor."

G. Washington

"We have no government armed with power capable of contending with human passions unbridled by morality and religion. Our Constitution was made only for a moral and religious people. It is wholly inadequate to the government of any other."

John Adams

IN GOD
WE TRUST

"And can the liberties of a nation be thought secure when we have removed their only firm basis, a conviction in the minds of the people that these liberties are the gift of God? That they are not to be violated but with His wrath? Indeed I tremble for my country when I reflect that God is just; that His justice cannot sleep forever."

Th Jefferson

"I've lived, sir, a long time, and the longer I live, the more convincing proofs I see of this truth: That God governs in the affairs of men. If a sparrow cannot fall to the ground without His notice, is it probable that an empire can rise without His aid? We've been assured in the sacred writings that unless the Lord builds the house, they labor in vain who build it."

Benj. *Franklin*

"America needs God more than God needs America.
If we ever forget that we are One Nation Under God, then we will be a Nation gone under."
- Ronald Reagan

BLESSED IS THE NATION WHOSE GOD IS THE LORD
Psalm 33:12

9

THE AMERICAN EXAMPLE

I n the last chapter we saw how a biblical worldview has made a difference in the way people live their lives. We've seen it personally, locally, in a country and in an entire culture. In this chapter I want to look specifically at how the biblical worldview has affected *our* country and particularly at how Christians have conducted themselves in the world of business. I believe that America's foundation on biblical principles is the primary element that led to our great success as a nation. The way I'd like to make this argument is to show you the lives of some Americans who made a difference in our country, and they did it by living out their biblical worldview.

Before we look at these folks, perhaps it would be helpful to hear about the exceptional nature of America from one of its most famous foreign observers.

ALEXIS DE TOCQUEVILLE
· · ·

Back in the early 1800s, Alexis de Tocqueville, a Frenchman, traveled across America during an extended visit. A historian and political journalist, de

Tocqueville was here primarily to examine our penal system, which required him to travel all over our country for nine months in 1831. When he returned to France, he published his findings in 1835 in a book titled *De la de'mocratie en Am'erique,* which was translated into English later that same year and titled *Democracy in America.* It is a deep and profound look at the early days of our nation, and it became a classic text used in history classes even to the present day.

De Tocqueville was so impressed with what he saw in America that he penned the following famous words: "The position of the Americans is quite exceptional, and it may be believed that no democratic people will ever be placed in a similar one."[35]

This was such a ringing endorsement from the Frenchman, and very soon the expression "American Exceptionalism" was coined. David Barton helped me to understand that this term was meant to describe the unique, distinctive ideas that were part of the American philosophy of government—ideas such as inalienable rights, individualism, limited government, full republicanism, separation of powers, checks and balances, and an educated and virtuous population.

De Tocqueville saw the connection between America's uniqueness and the influence of Christianity on that uniqueness. Just observe some of his writings concerning Christianity in our country:

> The greatest part of...America was peopled by men who...brought with them into the New World a form of Christianity which I cannot better describe than by styling it a democratic and republican religion. This sect contributed powerfully to the establishment of democracy and a republic, and from the earliest settlement of the emigrants politics and religion contracted an alliance which has never been dissolved.[36]

> [T]here is no country in the whole world in which the Christian religion retains a greater influence over the souls of men than in America; and there can be no greater proof of its utility, and of its conformity to human nature, than that its influence is most powerfully felt over the most enlightened and free nation of the earth.[37]

In the United States the influence of religion is not confined to the manners but it extends to the intelligence of the people.... Christianity therefore reigns without any obstacle—by universal consent.[38]

Religion in America takes no direct part in the government of society but it must nevertheless be regarded as the foremost of the political institutions of that country, for if it does not impart a taste for freedom, it facilitates the use of free institutions. Indeed, it is in this same point of view that the inhabitants of the United States themselves look upon religious belief. I do not know if all the Americans have a sincere faith in their religion, for who can search the human heart? But I am certain that they hold it to be indispensable to the maintenance of republican institutions. This opinion is not peculiar to a class of citizens or to a party but it belongs to the whole nation and to every rank of society.[39]

The Americans combine the notions of Christianity and of liberty so intimately in their minds that it is impossible to make them conceive the one without the other.[40]

I have known societies formed by the Americans to send out ministers of the Gospel into the new western states to found schools and churches there lest religion should be suffered to die away in those remote settlements, and the rising states be less fitted to enjoy free institutions than the people from which they emanated.... Thus religious zeal is perpetually stimulated in the United States by the duties of patriotism.[41]

Upon my arrival in the United States, the religious aspect of the country was the first thing that struck my attention; and the longer I stayed there, the more did I perceive the great political consequences resulting from this state of things, to which I was unaccustomed. In France, I had almost always seen the spirit of religion and the spirit of freedom pursuing courses diametrically opposed to each other, but in America I found that they were intimately united and that they reigned in common over the same country.[42]

It must never be forgotten that religion gave birth to...American society. In the United States, religion is therefore commingled with all the habits of the nation and all the feelings of patriotism.... [I]n America, religion has, as it were, laid down its own limits. Religious institutions have remained wholly distinct from political institutions so that former laws have been easily changed whilst former belief has remained unshaken. Christianity has therefore retained a strong hold on the public mind in America.... In the United States, Christian sects are infinitely diversified and perpetually modified; but Christianity itself is a fact so irresistibly established that no one undertakes either to attack or defend it.[43]

As David reminded me, "The Christian nature of America and its institutions was an aspect of American life and culture that de Tocqueville greatly admired. The fruits speak for themselves, even to the greatest of skeptics."

So who are some individual Americans who took these strong Christian values, this biblical worldview, and put it into action in the way they ran their businesses? We could write an entire book on the men and women who have followed God's Word in their business lives and as a result have prospered. Rather than record a long list of people with no time to explore their lives, let's look at two successful Christian businesspeople with a little greater depth and detail.

CYRUS MCCORMICK

· · ·

Reflecting on the life of Cyrus McCormick, his biographer Herbert Casson writes:

Cyrus McCormick was predestined, we may legitimately say, by the conditions of his birth, to accomplish his great work. From his father he had a specific training as an inventor; from his mother he had executive ability and ambition; from his Scotch-Irish ancestry he had the dogged tenacity that defied defeat; and from the wheat fields that environed his home came the call for the Reaper, to lighten the heavy drudgery of the harvest.[44]

Cyrus was born in 1809 on his parent's farm in rural Virginia. His father, Robert, had worked to invent a reaper from the time Cyrus was just a lad. But his father was not able to achieve success in the venture. From the time Cyrus was seven years old, his father tried one model after another, but to no avail. Robert's friends and neighbors began making fun of his failures, so the man began working in secret. No one was allowed in his workshop with the exception of his children. These secretive visits proved to be very inspirational to young Cyrus. That motivation, coupled with the physical demand of harvesting grain, proved to inspire the young man.

In July 1831, at twenty-two years of age, Cyrus McCormick demonstrated his first successful reaper on a small patch of wheat on his father's farm. A few days later he gave a public exhibition in the nearby town of Steele's Tavern. The observers were amazed and impressed as his reaper cut six acres of oats in one afternoon! To give that feat context, it is calculated that prior to his invention, the same production would have taken all afternoon—but with six laborers with scythes or twenty-four workers with sickles! Another calculation postulates that prior to the reaper, a farmer could harvest only one to three acres a day using a scythe. But with the reaper, a farmer and a helper could harvest *twelve* acres a day!

It should also be noted that many other people besides Cyrus's father attempted to invent a successful reaper. Cyrus was actually the forty-seventh person to apply for a patent for the invention. But his was the first that put everything together that was necessary for success. With an invention that significant, it would seem that the next events to record are filled with overwhelming success and popularity. But that was not the case. Actually it was *nine more years* of effort on his part to build a successful company that could produce the invention. More than once he came to the brink of bankruptcy, but due to his unwavering faith, dogged tenacity, and hard work, he made it through.

By the 1840s he was actually selling reapers. It didn't take long for him to realize that headquartering in Virginia was less than ideal, so he relocated his operation to a more centralized location: Chicago, Illinois. As he continued to look for new ways to sell his reaper, he is credited with developing a system of organization that revolutionized the way products were sold nationwide.

McCormick was brought up in a strong Christian home. However, it wasn't until Cyrus was twenty-five years old that he made a public profession of his faith. It was 1834 and Cyrus attended a series of meetings that were being held in a church that met on his grandfather's farm. Three ministers preached over four days, each of them inviting people to stand to their feet and acknowledge their faith. Biographer Herbert Casson recounted it this way:

> Cyrus McCormick was there, and he was not a member of the church, yet he did not stand up. That night his father went to his bedside and gently reproached him. "My son," he said, "don't you know that your silence is a public rejection of your Savior?" Cyrus was conscience stricken. He leapt from his bed and began to dress himself. "I'll go and see old Billy McClung," he said. Half an hour later, old Billy McClung, who was a universally respected religious leader in the community, was amazed to be called out of his sleep by a greatly troubled young man, who wanted to know by what means he might make his peace with his Maker. The next Sunday this young man stood up in church, and became in name what he already was by nature and inheritance—a Christian of the Presbyterian faith.[45]

McCormick's life exemplified a biblical worldview in every area, including business and work principles. One of the ideas he held to was the concept that business is a way of blessing and serving others. This selfless attitude is a far cry from the dog-eat-dog business world shown by more selfish executives. Stephen McDowell notes how blessing customers was actually carried out:

Cyrus built his business upon a number of unique ideas. One was a **written guarantee.** McCormick first "warranted the performance of the Reaper in every respect" in 1842, which helped him sell seven of them that year. In 1848, the guarantee was printed like an advertisement and if the machine did not perform according to the written agreement, he would take the machine back and refund the total price. This idea of a free trial and refund to dissatisfied customers was new then, but quite common today. This reflected the biblical ideas of serving and trusting the customer, seeking not chiefly personal profit, but providing the farmer with a machine that saved him labor and produced greater profit for him. He was caring for others and desired them to benefit from his invention.[46]

The invention of the reaper helped farmers in a way too wonderful for words. Yet Cyrus remained humble, faithful, and hard working throughout his entire life. He became a wealthy man, yet his wealth never caused him to lose his focus on his mission in life, given him by God.

McDowell summarizes this extraordinary life with these words:

> You do not have to be like Cyrus McCormick and invent something great to fulfill your divine mission. But as you are providing mankind with necessary goods or services and are helping to order and maintain God's creation, then that is sacred work. This can be done as a farmer, teacher, parent, manufacturer, carpenter, doctor, store clerk, etc.[47]

It has been estimated that at the time of his death, in 1884, enough grain was shipped from Chicago to bake *ten billion* loaves of bread a year, thanks to McCormick's invention. His company became the International Harvester Company in 1902.

Reflecting on McCormick's death, McDowell notes:

> The man who had faithfully done business and multiplied the talents God had given him—the man who had done so much to extend the

Kingdom of God on earth and who had reaped an abundance for himself, his family, and untold multitudes was now going to reap his external reward as a good and faithful servant.

May God grant us the grace to do business with the talents He has given us and to multiply them many-fold, so as to fulfill our divine purpose in the earth, and, to prepare us to rule and reign with Him forever.[48]

JOHN WANAMAKER

· · ·

Biographer Joseph Appel shares the following story about young John Wanamaker:

When John Wanamaker was a boy he went one Christmas Eve to a jewelry store in Philadelphia to buy his mom a gift. He said, "I had only a few dollars saved up for the purpose. I wanted to buy the best thing these dollars would buy. I guess I took a long time to look at the things in the jewelry cases. The jeweler was growing impatient. Finally I said, "I'll take that"—indicating a piece—just what it was I do not recall.

The jeweler began wrapping it up. Suddenly I saw another piece that I thought would better please my mother. "Excuse me, sir," I said, "but I have changed my mind. I'll take this piece instead of the one you are wrapping."

You can imagine my surprise and chagrin when the jeweler answered, "It's too late now. You've bought the first piece and you must keep it." I was too abashed to protest. I took what I had first bought, but as I went out of the store I said to myself, "When I have a store of my own the people shall have what they want...and what they ought to have."[49]

John Wanamaker was a strong Christian. From the very beginning, he built his business on a biblical worldview. Appel tells us that Wanamaker believed that "the Golden Rule of the New Testament has become the Golden Rule of business."[50] Some of Wanamaker's revolutionary concepts for his business included establishing a one price system, establishing the money back guarantee, the marking of the quality of goods, and the beginning the service-oriented store. He became known as the "father of modern advertising" due to the volume of advertising he would use for his stores. This practice drove his competitors to do the same, thus it gave birth to newspapers and magazines as we know them today, with the advertising making them affordable to all.

John was born into a Christian home near Philadelphia in 1838. His family had daily prayers together and often sang hymns together in the evenings. From an early age, John was a voracious reader. When he was eleven years old, he made the "most important purchase" (his words) of his life:

> In a little Mission Sunday School of the Lutheran Church, I bought from my teacher, Mr. Hurlbert, a small red leather Bible about eight inches long and six inches wide. The Bible cost $2.75 which I paid for in small installments as I saved up my own money that I had earned. Looking back over my life, that little red Bible was the foundation on which my life has been built, and it has made possible all that had counted most in my life. I know now that it was the greatest and most important and far reaching purchase I have ever made; and every other investment in my life seems, after mature years, only secondary.[51]

As a young man Wanamaker decided he would be a merchant, for he believed that was what God called him to do. While running his stores, however, he consistently gave himself to a wide variety of Christian ministries, including teaching Sunday school classes, teaching adult Bible classes, and the work of the Young Men's Christian Association, better known as the YMCA.

It is important to point out that because he was such a deeply committed Christian living in a country built on a biblical worldview, Wanamaker saw his Christian beliefs, his love of his country, and his business principles all bound together:

We are the pride of the nations of the world.... I feel as we cultivate holiness of heart and spread the glorious tidings of peace, inculcating the truth as it is in Jesus, so do we bind together our beloved Union. Inseparable with our prosperity is the religion of the Bible.[52]

"Inseparable with our prosperity is the religion of the Bible." Stephen McDowell refers to that phrase as John Wanamaker's life's creed.

In February 1861, John Wanamaker opened his first store with his partner (and brother-in-law) Nathan Brown. It was a men's clothing store that they called Oak Hill Clothing, situated at Sixth and Market Streets in the center of downtown Philadelphia. With it being the eve of the Civil War, it was not a good time to open a business selling men's clothes. But Wanamaker put his faith to work— he worked hard, served his customers, and pioneered the use of strategic advertising—and it brought him good success!

To John Wanamaker, godly principles were more important than profits. Integrity, honor, justice, and relating to his customers were the prime issues. Stephen McDowell, who has carefully studied the life of Wanamaker, observed:

The foundation of his business success was rooted in his Christian faith and character, for those produced the principles upon which he built his successful business, which included:

- Desire to please the customer, seen by returns accepted within ten days with money back (even for custom made items).
- One set price for all.
- He bought good quality items in quantity to get the lowest price, which he passed on to the customer.
- He marked the quality of goods so the customer could know what he was getting.
- He advertised extensively and used this to educate the consumer.
- He believed his service to the customer would be returned by loyalty of the customer to continue to return to buy goods.

- "The customer was right" was a foundational idea.
- At times he guaranteed a ten percent lower price than anywhere else.
- He established permanent buyers in European capitals of manufacturing.[53]

All of these innovations were surrounded by the concepts of hard work and perseverance. Wanamaker himself said:

> As I grow older, it becomes clearer to me that the difference between men who accomplish things and those who fail to accomplish things is in correct thinking, energy, and invincible determination. A single aim and a strong spirit, undistracted and untiring, seldom fall short of the goal. Work is master key to all the doors and opportunities. The man who never quits until the work is done inevitably writes his name on the roll of winners.[54]

When his partner died, Wanamaker continued his merchant ways on his own. In 1876 he purchased a large depot building that became known as the Grand Depot Store. It was the first department store in the nation.

In 1911 he moved the store right across the street from Philadelphia's famous city hall at Thirteenth and Market. The grand opening of the store, now simply called John Wanamaker's, was so noteworthy that the building was dedicated by the president of the United States, William Howard Taft. In his remarks, the president described the store as "one of the most important instrumentalities in modern life for the promotion of comfort among the people.... [It would be] a model for all other stores of the same kind throughout the world."[55]

To further emphasize the importance of the event, it should be observed that the ceremonies were attended by *thirty thousand people!*

The words on the dedication tablet said it all. If this store was to be successful it would be due to "freedom of competition and the blessing of God."[56]

Wanamaker himself underscored God as his ultimate source of success in his own remarks during the dedication ceremony:

I want to say, first of all, that one Hand alone has made it possible for us to have this day of felicity. That one Hand planted the forests, build into the hills the stone, laid down deep in the earth the iron, and through all the fifty years—beautiful years of dreaming and daring, but of health and of hope, of struggles and schooling, years the history of which it would be hard to write—plainly written over all these years, guiding and guarding, is the one signature of the good God, who is interested in us not only on Sundays, but on week days—the Father of us all, who cares for what we are doing. I want to say to the younger people coming on that it is poor prosperity that is blind to the need of God's favor, whether we are in business or out of it.[57]

The Philadelphia store would become the largest in the world. David Barton explained it to me this way: "It was much more than just its physical size. It had a spirit, a personality. The employee sought to serve the customer and had his well being in mind. The store entertained, educated, and performed special services. People enjoyed visiting, whether they bought items or not, and they were refreshed from the visit. Universities studied his stores to learn successful economic principles. They could see them at work. His success came from his character."

Wannamaker was a master at seeing how a businessman could view his business as a full-time ministry. His view was "religion first, earning power next, and a vision of general culture later.... I could accomplish more in the same domain if I became a merchant and acquire means and influence."[58]

Once he spoke to the Pierce Business School of Philadelphia, and a student asked him about success. Wanamaker replied:

I think it is possible for you to succeed because we came out from God, the source of life, to do something He fitted us for in the world He made for man, and the life He gave to each must go back to Him to give account of what the man did with it. I do not think He made us in His own image and likeness without meaning to help us to success, and we must admit the Creator surely has a right to elect His own way to do His work.[59]

John Wanamaker died on December 12, 1922, at his home in Philadelphia. William Jennings Bryan, the great American statesman and lawyer, called him:

America's greatest merchant...illustrating the possibilities in this land of the free.... His political career illustrates a high type of citizenship—he takes time for patriotic duties.... His personal life illustrates the beauty of Christian service.... Industry, undergirded by integrity, justice, morality, and fair dealings produced "the greatest merchant in the world."[60]

Before he died, a writer requested a sketch of his life. Wanamaker replied with typical wisdom: "Thinking, trying, toiling, and trusting in God is all of my biography."[61]

In those twelve words we see the life of a man who built his business upon a biblical worldview.

· · ·

John Wanamaker and Cyrus McCormick are just two examples of business people who approached their workaday world with a biblical worldview. We looked at these two men so we could highlight what an opportunity they had, not only because of their worldview, but also because they lived in America. Our Founding Fathers knew that if Americans could have the God-given right to prosper, prosper is what they would do. It is that freedom to thrive that has made our country great.

Yet many have chosen to wander away from our Christian heritage. By rejecting the biblical worldview, they have set a new course, going out on their own to do it a different way. Part of the freedom our country allows is for people to make their own choices and to live in different ways. But you will get a different result. Let's take a look at how that has played out in our country. •

THE WAY
in the manger!

But the angel said to them, "Do not be afraid. I bring you good news of great joy that will be for all the people. Today in the town of David a Savior has been born to you; he is Christ the Lord."
Luke 2:10-11 NIV

If you would like to know Jesus as Saviour and Lord, call the Need Him Ministry at 1-888-NEED HIM
If you are interested in Bible resources, visit www.scriptureresources.com

10

MOVING AWAY FROM OUR FOUNDATION

So far in this book we have attempted to spell out in some detail:

- how everyone has a worldview
- how our Founding Fathers came from a biblical worldview
- how their intention was that America would be a Christian nation
- there are good reasons to believe the Bible
- biblical guidelines are good for a society

In this chapter we will see how far things have moved away from our Founders' original intentions.

In an earlier chapter I uncovered ample evidence of our historical heritage, but perhaps some additional examples will serve us well. Dr. Benjamin Rush was one of the youngest signers of the Declaration of Independence; he was thirty-one years old in 1776. Rush was an accomplished physician and academic in the medical community as well as a patriot. John Adams described him as one of the three most notable Founders, ranking him along with George Washington and Benjamin Franklin. As president, Adams appointed Rush as treasurer of the U.S. Mint in 1797, a position Rush held until his death in 1813. It is also important to point out that Rush was a man of faith, a man who held the biblical worldview earnestly. Not only did he believe in the Bible, he was convinced it should be used as a textbook in the public schools. Lest there be any mistake about his convictions, here are portions of a letter he wrote in defense of the use of the Bible in the schools.

Dear Sir:

It is now several months since I promised to give you my reasons for preferring the Bible as a schoolbook to all other compositions. Before I state my arguments, I shall assume the five following propositions:

1. That Christianity is the only true and perfect religion; and that in proportion as mankind adopts its principles and obeys its precepts they will be wise and happy.
2. That a better knowledge of this religion is to be acquired by reading the Bible than in any other way.
3. That the Bible contains more knowledge necessary to man in his present state than any other book in the world.
4. That knowledge is most durable and religious instruction most useful, when imparted in early life.
5. That the Bible, when not read in schools, is seldom read in any subsequent period of life.

My arguments in favor of the use of the Bible as a schoolbook are founded:

I. In the constitution of the human mind.

1. The memory is the first faculty which opens in the minds of children. Of how much consequence, then, must it be to impress it with

the great truths of Christianity, before it is preoccupied with less interesting subjects.

2. There is a peculiar aptitude in the minds of children for religious knowledge. I have constantly found them, in the first six or seven years of their lives, more inquisitive upon religious subjects than upon any others.... It would be strange if it were otherwise, for God creates all His means to suit His ends.

3. ...The influence of early impressions is very great upon subsequent life and in a world where false prejudices do so much mischief, it would discover great weakness not to oppose them by such as are true. I grant than many men have rejected the impressions derived from the Bible, but how much soever these impressions may have been despised, I believe no man was ever early instructed in the truths of the Bible without having been made wiser or better by the early operation of these impressions upon his mind....

4. We are subject, by a general law of our natures, to what is called habit. Now if the study of the Scriptures be necessary to our happiness at any time of our life, the sooner we begin to read them, the more we shall probably be attached to them....

5. It is a law in our natures that we remember longest the knowledge we acquire by the greatest number of our senses. Now, a knowledge of the contents of the Bible is acquired in school by the aid of the eye and the ear....

6. The interesting events and characters recorded and described in the Old and New Testaments are calculated, above all others, to seize upon all the faculties of the mind of children. The understanding, the memory, the imagination, the passions, and the moral powers are all occasionally addressed by various incidents which are contained in those divine books, insomuch that not to be delighted with them is to be devoid of every principle of pleasure that exists in a sound mind.

7. There is in man a native preference of truth to fiction.... The Bible contains more truth than any other book in the world.... Indeed, my

friend, from some accounts which I have read of the American Revolution, I begin to grow skeptical to all history except that which is contained in the Bible....

8. There is a wonderful property in the memory which enables it in old age to recover the knowledge acquired in early life after it had been apparently forgotten for forty or fifty years. Of how much consequence then must it be to fill the mind with that species of knowledge in childhood and youth which, when recalled in the decline of life, will support the soul under the infirmities of age and smooth the avenues of approaching death. The Bible is the only book which is capable of affording this support to old age and it is for this reason that we find it resorted to with so much diligence and pleasure by such old people as have read it in early life.

II. My second argument in favor of the use of the Bible in schools is founded upon an implied command of God and upon the practice of several of the wisest nations of the world.

In the sixth chapter of Deuteronomy, we find the following words, which are directly to my purpose: "And thou shalt love the Lord thy God with all thine heart and with all thy soul and with all they might. And these words, which I command thee this day, shall be in thine heart. And thou shalt teach them diligently unto thy children and shalt talk of them when thou sittest in thy house and when thou walkest by the way, and when thou liest down, and when thou risest up."...

I wish to be excused from repeating here that if the Bible did not convey a single direction for the attainment of future happiness, it should be read in our schools in preference to all other books from its containing the greatest portion of that kind of knowledge which is calculated to produce private and public temporal happiness.[62]

There is much more to Rush's letter, but I think the point is well made with this section of it.

THE HISTORY OF THE BIBLE IN AMERICA[63]

• • •

As far back as 1647 the colonists in Massachusetts realized that it was vital to get the Bible into the hands of the common people. They felt so strongly about this issue, they put into effect a law known as the Old Deluder Satan Law of 1647. It is in an Old English style, but read it slowly in order to get the sense:

> It being one chief project of the old deluder, Satan, to keep men from the knowledge of the Scriptures, as in former times keeping them in an unknown tongue, so in these later times by persuading from the use of tongues, that so at least the true sense and meaning of the Original might be clouded by false glosses of Saint-seeming deceivers; and that learning may not be buried in the graves of our fore-fathers in Church and Commonwealth, the Lord assisting our endeavors: it is therefore ordered by this Court and Authority thereof:
>
> That every township in this jurisdiction, after the Lord hath increased them to the number of fifty householders, shall then forthwith appoint one within their town to teach all such children as shall resort to him to write and read, whose wages shall be paid either by the parents or masters of such children, or by the inhabitants in general, by way of supply, as the major part of those that order the prudentials of the Town shall appoint. Provided that those which send their children be not oppressed by paying much more than they can have them taught for in other towns.
>
> And it is further ordered, that where any town shall increase to the number of one hundred families or householders, they set up a Grammar School, the Masters thereof being able to instruct youth so far as they may be fitted for the University. And if any town neglect the performance hereof above one year then every such town shall pay five pounds per annum to the next such school, till they shall perform this Order.[64]

Many of the men we consider to be our Founding Fathers were passionate about the Scriptures being taught in the public schools. For example, Fisher

Ames helped frame the Bill of Rights, and he proposed the House version of the wording that we have today in the First Amendment. Ames wrote an article titled "Schoolbooks." What follows is an excerpt:

It has been the custom of late years to put a number of little books into the hands of children, containing fables and moral lessons. This is very well because it is right first to raise curiosity and then to guide it. Many books for children are, however, injudiciously complied. Why then, if these books for children must be retained, as they will be, should not the Bible regain the place it once held as a school book? Its morals are pure; its examples, captivating and noble. The reverence of the Sacred Book that is thus early impressed lasts long, and probably if not impressed in infancy, never takes firm hold of the mind.

A better-known Founding Father was our sixth president, John Quincy Adams. He was not only a statesman, but also an educator. He said: "To a man of liberal education...with regard to the history contained in the Bible...it is not so much praiseworthy to be acquainted with it as it is shameful to be ignorant of it."

One of the Founding Fathers who is usually categorized as less religious than his peers is Benjamin Franklin. Yet Franklin was responsible for reprinting *The New England Primer* in the state of Pennsylvania (we will discuss the primer shortly), and he was also one of the men who helped found the University of Pennsylvania. He spoke of his position regarding the university in a pamphlet titled *Proposals Relating to the Education of Youth in Pennsylvania.* Here is an excerpt: "History will...afford frequent opportunities of showing the necessity of a public religion from its usefulness to the public [and] the advantages of a religious character among private persons...and the excellency of the Christian religion above all others, ancient or modern."

Considered even less religious than Franklin was Thomas Paine. While lecturing in France, Paine made the following observations:

It has been the error of the schools to teach...sciences and subjects of natural philosophy as accomplishments only, whereas they should be taught...with reference to the Being who is the Author of them: for all the principles of science are of Divine origin.... When we examine an extraordinary piece of machinery, an astonishing pile of architecture, a well executed statue or a highly finished painting...our ideas are naturally led to think of the extensive genius and talents of the artist. When we study the elements of geometry, we think of Euclid. When we speak of gravitation, we think of Newton. How then is it, that when we study the works of God in the creation, we stop short and do not think of God? It is from the error of the schools...[and] the evil that has resulted...has been that of generating in the pupils a species of atheism. Instead of looking through the works of the creation to the Creator Himself, they stop short and employ the knowledge they acquire to create doubts of His existence.

It's important to understand that these men did more than just say these things. They saw to it that the Bible was taught in the schools *at all educational levels.*

At the elementary level, *The New England Primer* was first printed in 1690, and it was the first textbook printed in America. It became the most common text for teaching young students how to read for the next two hundred years. Three significant sections of the primer include: (1) The Rhyming Alphabet, (2) The Alphabet of Lessons for Youth, and (3) The Shorter Catechism. All three sections relied on the teachings of the Bible.

The Rhyming Alphabet began this way:

A — In Adam's Fall, We sinned all.
B — Heaven to find, the Bible to mind.
C — Christ crucified, for sinners died.

Each of the letters of the alphabet had a rhyme related to a Bible verse or doctrine.

The Alphabet of Lessons for Youth consisted of Bible verses that began with each of the successive letters:

- A wise son maketh a glad father, but a foolish son is the heaviness of his mother.
- Better is a little with the fear of the Lord, then great treasure and trouble therewith.
- Come unto Christ all ye that labor and are heavy laden and he will give you rest.

The Shorter Catechism is nothing less than the Westminster Confession of Faith, which was taught in the public school textbook for reading and studying!

At the high school level, consider that in the city of Dallas, Texas, they offered courses until 1974 that used textbooks titled *Bible Study Course, Old Testament, Dallas Public Schools* and *Bible Study Course, New Testament, Dallas Public Schools.* These texts were also used in major cities across the country, including St. Louis, Cincinnati, and Indianapolis. Not only did these courses outline the history of the Bible, but students were required to memorize Bible verses as part of the curriculum!

The teaching of the Bible didn't end at high school graduation, either. David Barton reports on two studies conducted in the 1800s. One study, from 1860, reported the following two amazing statistics:

- 262 of 288 college presidents were ministers of the Gospel
- Over one-third of the faculty at state universities were ministers of the Gospel.

James Angell, president of the University of Vermont and the University of Michigan, released the results of his *Survey of State Universities* in 1890. Among his findings:

- Over 90 percent of the universities he surveyed had chapel services

- 50 percent of the universities he surveyed had compulsory chapel attendance
- 25 percent of the universities he surveyed required church attendance in addition to chapel

There were many states that had written into their constitution the importance of religious education. The following is a portion of the Ohio state constitution from 1802: "Religion, morality, and knowledge, being essentially necessary to the good government and the happiness of mankind, schools and the means of instruction shall forever be encouraged by legislative provision."

That exact provision was included in the state constitutions for Mississippi, Kansas, Nebraska, and other states as well. That exact provision is *still* found in the state constitutions of North Carolina, Nebraska, and Ohio.

GETTING GOD OUT OF THE PICTURE
. . .

So what happened between our Founding Fathers and today? David French of the Alliance Defense Fund was in Oklahoma City recently, and I invited him to my office to sit down over a light lunch to discuss this topic with me. He graciously consented. Few people know the landscape of current American educational thought like he does, coupled with his firm grasp on our nation's history. Once we were settled in and had a chance to munch a little on our sandwiches, I posed the question to him about the difference between Benjamin Rush's ideas and what is going on today. "How do you explain it?" I asked.

"I will use my alma mater as an example in terms of answering that question," he replied thoughtfully. "I am a graduate of Harvard Law School. Harvard was founded in 1636. The original motto for the school was 'Truth for Christ and His Church" (in Latin). The logo for the school was three books, two facing us; opened, signifying knowledge we can know. The third book was opened, but facing away from us, signifying truth only God can know.

"But if you look at Harvard's motto and logo today, you will notice that some

FOR UNTO US A CHILD IS BORN
UNTO US A SON IS GIVEN
AND HIS NAME SHALL BE CALLED
WONDERFUL COUNSELOR
MIGHTY GOD
EVERLASTING FATHER
PRINCE OF PEACE

ISAIAH 9:6

changes have been made. I believe it was early in the twentieth century, close to the school's three hundredth anniversary, the powers that be chose to reduce the words of the motto to just one Latin word—*veritas*—meaning truth. They also took the third book and faced it toward us, like the other two, signifying that man can know all truth, essentially doing away with the necessity for God."

"So you are saying that the logo is symbolic of what has happened to our educational system," I concluded.

"Exactly. We've decided we have no need for God," David replied, shaking his head sadly.

"Where did thinking like that come from?" I asked.

"It's the influence we received from Europe," David replied. "By the end of the nineteenth century, the universities in Europe, most specifically Germany, had gone through a fairly major change in direction. They actually moved significantly from the traditional educational model that emphasized religious studies. Germany pioneered the model that a university should be a place for research, laboratories, and seminars. It wasn't too long after that we began to 'Germanize' our educational system, which is another way of saying we began to 'secularize' our system, to dramatically deemphasize religious instruction."

"The academics just pushed God out of the way, didn't they?" I scratched my head, not knowing why men and women of such seeming intelligence would make such an unwise decision.

"Also, don't forget," David reminded me, "you cannot overstate the importance of World War I on education."

"What's the connection?" I asked.

"The war killed Christianity in Europe. All the slaughter, all the killing led by people who claimed Christian foundations—it was overwhelming. The faith in traditional institutions just died. Out of World War I came Communist Russia and soon after came Fascist Italy and Germany."

"But that's Europe, not us," I interjected.

"True. Yet even though the average American seemed unaffected by what was going on in Europe, it was deeply impacting the American academic community. Through books, journals, magazines, and other writings from the

European professors, before too long the American educational system would be influenced to create the same kinds of movements."

"And what affects the academics ultimately affects us, right?" I summarized.

"That's exactly right, Steve. My friend and colleague Jeff Ventrella refers to it as 'the robes of culture.' The robes of academia influence those who go on to become lawyers and one day wear the robes of judges. They will interpret the laws, and then the ministers will go along with what they are saying, so that brings in the robes of clergy. That's precisely what happened here in the United States. Think of the radical students who started springing up on university campuses—they graduated and eventually became professors at those very same schools. While other graduates became judges and still others became clergy. All together they make up the robes of culture."

"So the changes we saw in our legal system in the 1960s that impacted education were really the tip of the iceberg," I said.

"Those changes happened due to years and years of work. Just think of how long it takes to gain control in the Supreme Court! Yes, the decade of the Sixties was a real heyday for everything from striking down prayer and Bible reading in the public schools to the free speech movement to the whole zealous effort to establish the separation of church and state. But it began long before that time."

1962: NO MORE PRAYER IN THE PUBLIC SCHOOLS
• • •

While recently researching the decision of the U.S. Supreme Court to do away with prayer in the public schools, I was amazed at the dissenting opinion written by Justice Potter Stewart. Consider some of the things he wrote in that opinion:

> A local school board in New York has provided that those pupils who wish to do so may join in a brief prayer at the beginning of each school day, acknowledging their dependence upon God and asking His blessing upon them and upon their parents, their teachers, and their country. The Court today decides that, in permitting this brief nondenominational

prayer, the school board has violated the Constitution of the United States. I think this decision is wrong....

With all respect, I think the Court has misapplied a great constitutional principle. I cannot see how an "official religion" is established by letting those who want to say a prayer say it. On the contrary, I think that to deny the wish of these school children to join in reciting this prayer is to deny them the opportunity of sharing in the spiritual heritage of our nation....

We deal here, not with the establishment of a state church, which would, of course, be constitutionally impermissible, but with whether school children who want to begin their day by joining in prayer must be prohibited from doing so. I think the Court's task, in this as in all areas of constitutional adjudication is not responsibly aided by the uncritical invocation of metaphors like the "wall of separation," a phrase nowhere to be found in the Constitution. What is relevant to the issue here is not the history of an established church in sixteenth century England or in eighteenth century America, but the history of the religious traditions of our people, reflected in countless practices of the institutions and officials of our government.

At the opening of each day's Session of this Court, we stand, while one of our officials invokes the protection of God. Since the days of John Marshall, our Crier has said, "God save the United States and this Honorable Court." Both the Senate and the House of Representatives open their daily sessions with prayer. Each of the presidents from George Washington to John Kennedy [remember, this dissent was written in 1962, during Kennedy's administration] has, upon assuming his Office, asked the protection and help of God.

The Court today says that the state and federal governments are without constitutional power to prescribe any particular form of words to be recited by any group of the American people on any subject touching religion. One of the stanzas of "The Star Spangled Banner" made our National Anthem by Act of Congress in 1931, contains these verses:

Blest with victory and peace, may the heaven rescued land,
Praise the Power that hath made and preserved and made us a nation.
Then conquer we must, when our cause it is just,
And this be our motto, "In God is our Trust."

In 1954, Congress added a phrase to the Pledge of Allegiance to the Flag so it now contains the words "one Nation, under God, indivisible, with liberty and justice for all." In 1952, Congress enacted legislation calling the President each year to proclaim a National Day of Prayer. Since 1865, the words "In God We Trust" have been on our coins.

Countless similar examples could be listed, but there is no need to belabor the obvious. It was all summed up by this Court just ten years ago in a single sentence: "We are a religious people whose institutions presuppose a Supreme Being."

I do not believe that this Court, or the Congress, or the President, has, by the actions and practices I have mentioned, established an "official religion" in violation of the Constitution. And I do not believe the state of New York, has done so in this case. What each has done has been to recognize and to follow the deeply entrenched and highly cherished spiritual traditions of our nation—traditions which come down to us from those who almost two hundred years ago avowed their "firm Reliance on the Protection of divine Providence" when they proclaimed the freedom and independence of this brave new world.

I dissent.[65]

It's almost hard to imagine that there were justices on the Supreme Court who would take that sort of stand back in the Sixties. There were a few, but obviously not enough to stand against the turning tide of those days. In some ways it felt like a snowball rolling down a hill—it just kept gaining in momentum.

Which brings us to today. So let's take a look at the situation involving Emily Brooker.

EMILY BROOKER

. . .

The true account of Emily Brooker is a singular illustration of how far the U.S. educational system has strayed from the original ideals of the Founding Fathers (like we saw in the letter from Dr. Benjamin Rush). I first became aware of Emily's situation through the information provided to me by the Alliance Defense Fund Center for Academic Freedom. And again, one of their finest legal minds, my friend David French, was very much involved in the case.

"Our institutions of higher learning have to be very far gone before you can even have a case like Emily Brooker's," David commented in a recent interview. "The case occurred because we have an ideological monoculture on our campuses today. It's one idea that's the truth—the leftist idea. Not only can your alternative idea not be heard, but you're going to have to *vocalize* the left idea in order to receive your degree."

In a sad but honest conclusion, David reflected, "It's hard to get more un-American than that."

Emily Brooker was in the second semester of her senior year at Missouri State University. She was only months away from graduating with a degree in social work. The professor in her Policy 2 class made an assignment that changed Emily's life by challenging her beliefs and convictions. The assignment was to become an advocate—that sounded innocent enough, even kind of exciting. But when the issue was announced as to what they would advocate, Emily began to wonder how she could get through his class without compromising her beliefs?

She was assigned to be an advocate for homosexual adoption.

The original assignment itself was not the problem. It was a class assignment to argue for a position, no different than in a law class, where the class is divided into two groups, each charged with arguing opposing sides. You may not agree with the side you were assigned, but you still were arguing the case in class.

The problem for Emily was what she was asked to do at the end of the assignment. She was told to sign a paper in order to lobby the state legislature for the cause that she did not believe in. She was told that if she didn't sign the paper, she would fail. In simple terms, that is *coercion*.

Emily said, "My heart just sank."

After the class, she told the teacher, "I can't advocate for this on a political level. It is against my beliefs and I'm not going to do it."

"Is it because you are a Christian?" the professor inquired as he continued to press the issue with her.

"I am a Christian," Emily replied, "and that does guide me, but this is a right or wrong issue!"

David French wisely interjected at this point: "The President of the United States cannot walk into a classroom and say, 'You must advocate in favor of my policies.' We can say, 'Respectfully, Mr. President, I decline to do that.' What makes a social work professor think he can do what the president of the United States cannot? But that is the level of arrogance we deal with all too often on college campuses today."

Things began to intensify for Emily. She was brought alone into a room where she was asked to sit at one side of a long rectangular table. Across from her were no less than *seven* professors from the university.

"They asked me unbelievably intrusive questions," Emily remembers. They asked her many questions specifically related to her faith.

"Are homosexuals sinners?" they asked.

"Are *you* a sinner?"

"Are *we* sinners?"

"What's the difference?"

Emily recalled the session as "tough...intimidating. There were times that I cried." But she was resolute. "I wanted them to know I wasn't going to change my mind."

The meeting went on for *two and half hours!*

Finally, the professors concluded: "You need to continue to educate yourself about the homosexual lifestyle, and you need to write a paper on how you will lessen the gap between your personal beliefs and your professional obligations."

Emily's parents were just outside the room during this meeting. They were praying. When Emily came out and recounted what had taken place, her parents knew it was time to take action. "We called David French of the Alliance

Defense Fund," Emily's mother recalled, "because we believe people need to know that these sorts of things are going on in college classrooms."

Thanks to the work of the attorneys at the Alliance Defense Fund, Emily was able to graduate without compromising her Christian beliefs. A lawsuit was filed against the university. To the academic institution's credit, it made the necessary changes to the department to keep this issue from ever happening again. The matter was ultimately settled out of court. But the fact remains, it took lawyers to make it happen, and that is a sad commentary on the public education system of the United States.

By far the majority—67 percent at last count[66]—of our public universities have speech codes that either restrict or prohibit constitutionally protected free speech. Dozens of colleges have tried to throw Christian student groups off campus. Our education system is a stark reminder of how America has moved away from its foundation.

The Bible, a primary source our Founding Fathers looked to in establishing our country, has gone from being openly taught in the public schools to being eliminated to the point that student have to espouse a view they do not embrace in order to graduate. There are other cases like Emily's in the courts, and who knows how many cases there could be if people knew that help was available. •

The Promise in the manger,

"And if Christ has not been raised, our preaching is useless and so is your faith."
1 Corinthians 15:14 NIV

Fullfilled in an empty tomb.

"Praise be to the God and Father of our Lord Jesus Christ! In His great mercy He has given us new birth into a living hope through the resurrection of Jesus Christ from the dead..."
1 Peter 1:3 NIV

He is risen!

If you would like to know Jesus as Saviour and Lord, call the Need Him Ministry at 1-888-NEED HIM.
If you are interested in Bible resources, visit www.scriptureresources.com.

Hobby Lobby, Mardel & Hemispheres Stores • 7707 S.W. 44th Street • Oklahoma City, OK 73179 • www.hobbylobby.com

11

PUTTING IT ALL TOGETHER

Clearly, we have moved away from the intentions of our forefathers. In the previous chapter we saw how this has played out in the public education system. The answer to the question, What are we to teach our children? has changed radically from what the Founders had put in place.

As a country we are moving away from the intentions of our Founding Fathers in many other areas as well. Questions are being asked and the answers are different from what they used to be. What will be the determining factors in coming up with answers? As we have been discussing, our worldview determines how we answer today's questions. This forces us to ask: Is there a worldview that is right and others wrong? Can we coexist with different worldviews? Do we have to have a worldview at all? If we have to have a worldview what worldview will we use to decide the questions that we have to answer collectively as a society?

I believe our forefathers, time and time again, would look to the Bible and it was from a biblical worldview that they answered the questions they faced. I have worked hard to demonstrate this fact throughout the book and I hope you see that possibility from the mountain of quotes from the Founding Fathers, as well as testimony from the experts.

Paul Harvey regularly said, "Self-government without self-discipline won't work." The self-discipline he talked about is the discipline to do what is right even though we may have the desire to do otherwise. It is a moral code by which we strive to live. That moral code, the determination of what is right and wrong, comes from our worldview. We all have to personally make a decision of what is right and wrong and we make that decision collectively as well through the laws we pass.

I have attempted to show that a society has a worldview as the foundation on which its laws are built. Everyone can choose his or her own worldview, but it is not possible for all of us to have our own worldview and fully coexist. When worldviews differ in what is believed to be right and wrong one will win out.

It is no more possible to coexist than for everyone to drive by his or her own rules. Granted, we have the freedom to buy whatever car we may desire and afford. If safety is an issue, we can buy a safe car. If fuel economy is a concern, we can purchase accordingly. We can pick size and color. We have the freedom to drive with the windows down, the radio on, add cool hubcaps, or a personalized license plate. In that sense, we can all be different and coexist.

But no one has the freedom to decide that a red light means go. If you happen to be from Great Britain, you don't get to decide to drive on the left side of the road. There is no coexisting on these matters. There are some things that we are not free to do. For the good of our society, we have collectively decided what is best for our society. Acceptance of the rules is required, whether you happen to like the rules or not.

That's why to say our government shouldn't have a religion is counterintuitive. A religion is a moral code and a government establishes a moral code by the laws it passes. The real question is, On what moral code or worldview is the government going to be established?

A government without a God or based on an atheistic worldview has proven to lead to tragic consequences. I have sought to demonstrate that a worldview of that nature is built on junk science, and furthermore it has created the most dangerous forms of government. As has been said by one cynic, "If you think I am bad with religion, you should see me without religion!"

So the question remains, which worldview will we look to in order to determine what our laws will allow and prohibit? Will we look to the Bible as our Forefathers did, or do we decide to go a different direction?

It is said that you cannot legislate morality, yet that is exactly what every law does! Stealing and murder are wrong, so we have laws against them. But the law is limited. Just because we pass a law that makes stealing illegal doesn't change the heart of the thief. The law doesn't change a person's morality, so in that sense you cannot legislate morality, but it does establish what a society believes is moral. At the heart of a government's responsibility is to determine what is right and wrong through its laws and then reward good and punish evil. The government rewards good by not interfering with its citizens' God-given freedoms, their inalienable rights, and by creating just laws by which all should live. It punishes evil by enforcing those laws that have been broken—even to the point of sending people to prison if required.

Obviously there is something wrong with a government that punishes good and rewards evil. If a law encourages immoral behavior or punishes good behavior it is counterproductive for a society. When a society passes laws, the people are saying what they believe to be right and wrong. Some laws can be passed that are pretty much universally accepted but there will be some laws that will favor one worldview over another. The question for America is which worldview will be used?

By now it should be clear that I believe the Bible gives human beings the guidelines by which we should live. This is not because of a personal preference, or even because they work. It is because I believe they are the guidelines our Creator, the loving God, gave to us. He gave them to us because He loves us and wants the best for us. To the degree in which a society follows those guidelines is the degree to which that society lives well. If a society wants to ignore biblical guidelines for living, it can choose to do so, but it will suffer the consequences.

As a business Hobby Lobby strives to follow biblical principles even though at times they don't seem to make sense. We do that because we believe in the long run it will provide the best results that are not measured only by monetary measurements. I believe them to be the best for me and for others as well. We could keep them to ourselves but why? Why would we keep to ourselves what we believe is the source of our success? Not to share it would be selfish, a violation of the very instructions we are striving to follow.

We live in a free country and we are free to offer to you something for your consideration. We believe it is the greatest source of peace, joy, and hope one could ever know. The Bible tells us that God created mankind and that He gave us the choice to serve Him to disobey Him. Man chose to disobey. When Jesus Christ was here on earth, He gave instructions to His disciples to go and tell the good news to all people. The good news is that God has provided a solution for our disobedience. He offers us the choice to accept it or not. That is the essence of the message of the Bible. Should you trust this book? I believe so but again that choice is yours.

Understanding more about this book might be helpful. The Bible is a book like no other. Over forty writers wrote it over approximately fifteen hundred years. It was written by people from all walks of life: peasants, kings, philosophers, fishermen, poets, statesmen, and scholars, to name a few. It was written by rich and poor, young and old, during times of joy and despair, war and peace, on three different continents, in three different languages and yet it is a book that answers all the big questions of life and deals with innumerable controversial subjects harmoniously.

Though it is not a history book in a traditional sense, it accurately tells of the past as it has and will the future. Compared with other ancient writings, the Bible has more manuscript evidence than the manuscript evidence for *all* of the major classical works *combined* many times over! No document of the ancient period is as well attested bibliographically as the Bible.

Many academics have tried to discredit it through Higher Criticism and yet time and time again further discoveries prove the critics wrong. Many have tried to burn it, ban it, and outlaw it, yet it is the bestselling book every year and of all times. The Bible has been read by more people and published in more languages than any other book. There is absolutely no book that reaches or even begins to compare to its circulation.

But God demonstrates His own love toward us, in that while we were still sinners, Christ died for us.

HE DIED. WE LIVE.

Much more then, having now been justified by His blood, we shall be saved from wrath through Him.
— Romans 5:8-9

It is a book that analyzes while being analyzed. It has the power to turn the hard soft, the angry loving, and the anxious calm. It is the book that has had a greater impact on this earth than any other book. It is a book that has changed the world. It is a book that is alive because it is the revelation of the living God.

The main character of the book is a man who was born in an obscure village, the child of a young, unwed peasant woman. He grew up in another village where He worked in a carpenter's shop until He began His ministry. Then for around three years He was an itinerant preacher.

He never owned a home. He never wrote a book. He never held an office. He never had a family. He didn't go to college. He never traveled two hundred miles from the place He was born. He did none of the things usually associated with greatness. He had no credentials but Himself.

Then shortly into His ministry the tide of popular opinion turned against him. His friends ran away. One of them denied Him. He was turned over to His enemies. He went through the mockery of a trial. He was nailed upon a cross between two thieves. While He was dying His executioners gambled for the only piece of property He had on earth—His coat. When He was dead, He was laid in a borrowed grave through the pity of a friend.

Twenty long centuries have come and gone, and today He is the central figure of the human race and the leader of human progress.

It is fair to say that all the armies that ever marched, all the navies that were ever built; all the parliaments that ever sat and all the kings that ever reigned, put together, have not affected the life of man on this earth as powerfully as has that *One Solitary Life*.[67]

And He is the reason we do what we do. We believe in Jesus Christ and His written word to us. We believe He loves us and has directed us in how we should live. We believe it is worthy for your consideration and for the consideration of our nation. We believe that in the Bible are the words of life—an abundant life. It is not a life free of trouble, but it is a life of peace, joy and hope that cannot be fully explained.

It is time for our nation to make a decision on what direction it is going to take. Just like the children of Israel in the Old Testament were challenged on several occasions to make a choice: either serve the God that brought them to where they were or turn to the other gods. That is the same choice America faces and we all individually face. It is a decision we will always be faced with both as a nation and individually. I pray that you will make the wise decision individually and we as a nation will make the wise decision collectively. •

Beyond
the shadow

of the
Cross...

HE LIVES!

He is not here.

HE HAS RISEN

just as he said...

Matthew 28:6

12

NOT ALL LETTERS
WE RECEIVE ARE CRITICAL

At Hobby Lobby, we have done our best at creating an answer to the letters that were critical of our ads. It was never our intention to jam anything down anyone's throat or try to be controversial. Ours is a biblical worldview, and we wanted to state it in an open manner. Remember, when I began this book with letters of criticism, we had received *forty-one* critical letters out of a total of *five hundred thirty-one*!

In order to end this story on an upbeat note, I thought I would share with you some of the most inspiring letters we have received over the years. We have had letters delivered to us about our Christmas ads, our Easter ads, our Fourth of July ads, our policy of being closed on Sundays, letters about the kind of music we play in our stores, the way our stores are designed, and every subject imaginable. What follows is only a sampling, but it will give you a better idea and a broader picture of a typical day's mail at our Oklahoma City headquarters:

To Whom It May Concern:

I want to thank your company for the wonderful ad in the *Shreveport Times* on July 4th, 2009. (I have shared with many and have carried it around with me for several days!) What better day than Independence Day to put this wonderful information for all to know that our Founding Fathers and Leaders were Godly men. We are a Christian nation, unlike what has been said recently by our leaders. If we do not get back to those basics of our humble and Christian beginnings, then I believe that our country is in great danger.

I read an article today [from another group] in response to your ad and I have to admit I was angered by it. She was shaming the *Times* for printing it. America has opened up its arms to all nationalities and beliefs, but our beginnings are based on Christianity. We should have the right to express this. If [the other group] wants to buy a full-page ad to tell about their faith or whatever then so be it. Good grief! It is their First Amendment right to do so as given to them through our United States Constitution. I admire your company for this and I will definitely be patronizing your wonderful store now more than ever. God bless you and God bless America.

· · ·

Dear Hobby Lobby:

Thank you. Thank you! The July 4th full-page ad/message in our local paper was absolutely awesome, encouraging, inspiring—it should have been on the front page instead of 5–6 pages back! Thank you for honoring our Lord by being closed on Sundays, for playing Christian music in your stores and by making a public statement on the importance of a personal relationship with Christ on various holidays in the local paper. It gives Christians in our community even more boldness/courage to speak out and take a stand regarding faith in Christ. Blessings to you and yours.

Letter to the Editor:

I have always been so impressed with the ads that Hobby Lobby sponsors in your newspaper around certain holidays and Independence Day weekend was no exception. Their full-page, full-color ad highlighting the Christian values of our American heritage was a keeper.

In this day and age of expected tolerance for every conceivable group, it seems increasingly rare for Christians to receive the same level of public respect in return. Public censorship of Christian morals has left its mark on our society. Our God is a God of love, grace and forgiveness, but He is also our final judge.

These are the values this country was built upon. Thanks to Hobby Lobby and other brave followers of Christ, we can be reminded of that truth periodically. May God truly bless America!

· · ·

Dear Hobby Lobby:

Since my husband works for a competitor I do not shop often at other craft/fabric stores. I have a small sewing/craft business in my home; we make and sell a specific product at craft malls and shows. I was VERY impressed with Hobby Lobby's Christmas '98 newspaper ad, it is the reason I decided to check out the Web site. I am also impressed with your statement and goals; the fact that you don't use your Christian commitment to draw customers in any way, solidifies a positive image of the company in my mind. I will be recommending Hobby Lobby even more than I have previously.

As a businessperson, I prefer Hobby Lobby stores for the neat, clean, organized appearance combined with selection and competitive pricing. I know what it takes to keep a store looking good and well stocked and I commend you for doing both better than your competition (in my opinion).

Dear Hobby Lobby,

I have owned a restaurant in Waterloo, IA for a little over three years. Until recently, my business was open seven days a week. However, I felt the Lord was telling me I should honor Him by being closed on Sundays. I had no doubt it was the right thing to do, but with the competition being open Sundays and not knowing how my customers would react did worry me somewhat. Your decision to close your first Waterloo Hobby Lobby store on Sunday helped reinforce my decision to do the same and, effective December 27, my business is no longer open on Sunday. The Lord has blessed me with my business in my first three years and I trusted that He would continue to do so, even without the Sunday sales. I have not been disappointed. He continues to provide more than I could have asked or expected. After all, "my" business is really His business. Thank you for taking a stand for Christ, something often lacking in the business world today. I also want to thank you for the inspirational full-page ad you placed in the *Waterloo Courier* at Christmastime.

Please pass my comments along to the Board of Directors so they know of the support they have from other Christian business owners of their decision to honor our Lord in their business dealings.

• • •

Dear Hobby Lobby:

Thank you very much for putting the Easter picture in the newspaper! I like it a lot.

Love Elisha

PS: Yes, He lives in my heart!

[Elisha is ten years old and hand-printed this letter to us, complete with a drawing of a cross and a heart.]

Son,
I need you to
Build
a Bridge;
here are all the
tools you will need.
See you soon –

Love,
Dad

©2003 KERUSSO.COM

"That's what Christ did definitively; suffered
because of others' sins, the Righteous One
for the unrighteous ones. He went through
it all, was put to death and then made alive
to bring us to God."
1 Peter 3:18, The Message

Dear Friends:

Just a few words to express our thankfulness for your ad in the *Joliet Herald News*. We appreciate your willingness to proclaim Christ on Easter Sunday. Obviously a full-page ad costs a great deal. Thank you!

Enclosed is a sheet that some of the people at our church signed to express their gratitude as well.

Blessings on you.

[The letter above came from the pastor of a local church and was accompanied by a paper signed by eighty-seven members of their congregation!]

. . .

Dear Mr. Green:

As a consumer, a Christian, and a State legislator, I want to express my personal appreciation for your outstanding Easter message as displayed in the full-page advertisement in the Fort Wayne, Indiana *Journal Gazette*.

It is not often that even an organization owned and/or run by Christians is willing to expend the energy and resources to declare the Truth of the Gospel in such unmistakable terms.

As the owners of a growing, 30-year-old business ourselves (we service major chain retailers with Fourth of July sparklers and novelty assortments in 20 states), my father, brother, and I sincerely appreciate it when we see other companies doing their best to perform with excellence *and* to share their faith. We also realize that when that happens, others begin to more closely examine our business, and our lives, to see if they are consistent with biblical principles and godly character. Your willingness to open yourselves in this fashion is exemplary.

We are only beginning to learn more about Hobby Lobby (and had not heard of Mardel Stores), but from what we see in our home area your business is certainly one with which to be pleased. Our prayer is that God will bless and strengthen you in your mission, in your business, and in your families.

Because He Lives you can have eternal life.

If you confess with your mouth the Lord Jesus, and believe in your heart that God has raised Him from the dead, you shall have eternal life.

-paraphrased from Romans 10:9

To Whom It May Concern:

Due to illness I was unable to attend an Easter service yesterday and was disappointed. But when my husband showed me your full-page ad declaring essentially the true message of Easter "He Lives," I felt like I'd been to church. Thank you for this bold expression of Truth and investing the expense. Please consider me a vocal supporter in every way possible of Hobby Lobby stores.

· · ·

Dear Sirs:

I have intended to write your company since Sunday, April 12th, after I saw your *full-page* advertisement quoting the Bible scripture of Romans 10:9 in the *Saint Joseph News Press* newspaper, Saint Joseph, Missouri. In fact, I remember that last year you also had a full-page ad at Eastertime like the one this year.

Yes, Jesus does live within my heart! This is the question your article asked at the bottom of the page and I am proud to answer this question.

In the *Saint Joseph News Press* a few days ago, on Sunday, they have a section on their Opinion Page for "Your Bouquets" where people can call or write in and I am enclosing a small section that someone had sent in about your full-page ad this Easter. I'm sure there were a lot of people who felt the same inspiration when they opened their paper Easter morning and saw your ad.

Thank you very much for this wonderful ad and inspirational verse. God bless your company.

[Enclosed with this letter was a small clipping from their newspaper: Your Bouquets—To Hobby Lobby for the inspiring full-page ad in the paper on Easter Sunday.]

Good Morning:

I must tell you how much your full-page ad in the *Kansas City Star* on Easter morning meant to me and my wife.

We are involved in publishing Gospel tracts to be used in witnessing. Established in 1926 as a not-for-profit, non-denominational ministry, we publish millions of tracts each year. Sometimes, though, I get the feeling that we are the only ones burdened for the souls of lost men and women.

To see the bold type proclaiming that "No One Empties A Tomb Like Jesus" in a major metropolitan newspaper lets me know that we are not alone in the effort to win the lost.

My wife's response to the ad was to say, "Now I know why I have always enjoyed shopping there!"

Again, thank you for your boldness in proclaiming Jesus as Savior. I am confident that God will bless your efforts and your business. Please call on us if we can help you in any way in the future.

· · ·

My Friends:

I am Adrian Rogers. I have served three terms as President of the Southern Baptist Convention, which is the world's largest evangelical denomination.

I only tell you that to let you know that I believe I speak for literally millions who appreciate the advertisement that was found in newspapers like the *Commercial Appeal,* that is published in Memphis, Tennessee.

The full-page, displayed ad carries a headline title that says, "No one empties a tomb like Jesus." Then, a Scripture verse taken from Romans 10:9.

Hobby Lobby and Mardel Stores, who sponsored the ad, were discreetly referenced at the bottom of the page.

I sincerely want to thank you for this bold witness and for the courage and the expenditure that it took to make such a witness. On behalf of many of us, I say a sincere thank you and trust that Hobby Lobby and Mardel Stores will continue to set this standard.

. . .

Hobby Lobby and Mardel Stores:

I am enclosing copy a of a letter I wrote to the *Kansas City Star* regarding your full-page Christmas Day ad in their paper.

I was a child of the Depression and was raised on high moral and religious standards. I've been dismayed to see those standards sink as low as they are in our country today.

Your ad was tasteful and delightful, and got the point across without preaching (which people nowadays resist). To me, it was like the gates of Heaven opened up and God shouted, "I'm still here." Certainly, He was in the hearts of those who originated, produced, and designed this beautiful ad. Our country needs reminding, and you did so beautifully.

God bless you. And I know He will.

[Enclosed with the above letter was a copy of the following letter she wrote to the *Kansas City Star*]

I seldom have praise for advertising in any newspaper, but I'd like to commend the full-page ad in the *Kansas City Star* on Christmas Day by Hobby Lobby and Mardel Stores.

Too often, we forget the true meaning of Christmas. And for the reminder to come in a tasteful, paid, full-page ad was refreshing and encouraging.

This company exhibited true leadership. I hope their example will be followed by others to return our country to the high morals and beliefs that our forefathers had.

Dear Mr. President:

Today as we were singing "Tell It Out with Gladness" in our worship service, the Holy Spirit nudged me again to write you a letter of thanks and appreciation. My heart was so glad when I opened up our local paper, the *Jonesboro Sun* on Christmas Day and saw your full-page ad. I knew then I must let you know how refreshing it was on that day we celebrate our Lord and Savior's birth, to see and read your ad alongside all the other news in the paper. And not just a small square in the corner but large enough that everyone who read the paper would see it. Thank you. Thank you. Thank you.

> "Lord, we thank thee for the treasure
> Hid within the sacred page.
> We would by thy faithful heralds
> To our deeply troubled agd.
> We would publish thy salvation
> Ever on thy side to stand.
> Living, serving, giving,
> Sending Life to quicken every land."

There was a confirmation in my spirit as we sang this second verse that I must tell you of the encouragement that ad was to me on Christmas Day. Thank you, Hobby Lobby, for your faithful *herald* in this truly deeply troubled age we live in. Thank you for *publishing* God's salvation and I pray it will send life to many lands.

You will find this grandmother of four from Jonesboro, Arkansas walking through the doors of Hobby Lobby often. Thank you again.

• • •

Dear Mr. Green:

My family members are big fans of your stores. We not only enjoy shopping in your stores because of your products, but also because of the wonderful Christian music you have played in every store no matter where we shop. We applaud your work and your Christian values.

Thank you for being courageous and displaying your faith for all to see.

Thank you for being a man of conviction and being unashamed of being a Christian company!

God bless you.

· · ·

Dear Friends:

One of the things I most appreciate about Hobby Lobby is the open Christian witness that the company takes. I love shopping to hymns in the background. I encourage all my friends to shop at Hobby Lobby.... *I tell them it's almost like tithing.*

Thanks for your testimony. It makes me happy to give you my business.

· · ·

Dear Hobby Lobby,

Sometimes I could just wring your neck when you're not open on Sundays! But I appreciate your stand and I mean that...and I really like the Christian music that plays in our store in Baytown. I can't tell you how much I like to shop around and listen to that, instead of some secular stuff elsewhere.

· · ·

To Whom It May Concern:

I am writing to express my sincere admiration for your decision to close on Sundays. It is very inspiring in this day and age to see a company, such as yourself, more concerned with spiritual issues than with the bottom line. Don't get me wrong, I understand you stand to lose a great deal of money. The last figure I read was around 100 million a year. I am also aware of who made this decision, though I don't know their names.

I am sure that top-level executives struggled with this decision and I am sure that you have and will continue to take a lot of criticism. I also realize that these executives who made this decision were already able to attend worship services on Sunday. This is what impresses me even more. That you have decided to put 100 million dollars aside in order to enable your employees at the front line to attend worship services. I have to confess, I have never been to your store, and yet hundreds of dollars in checks every month are written to Hobby Lobby out of my checkbook. You see, my wife shops there frequently. I used to be irritated by this. I want you to know that she now has my full blessing, and I also want you to know that you now have my prayers. I pray that God will bless your company with incredible profits and that this will start a huge trend in our society. Thank you very much. Please see to it that those executives who made this decision see this letter.

· · ·

Dear Hobby Lobby,

I wanted to write and tell you that thanks to your Easter message my makeup was a mess on Easter Sunday morning.

I got all ready for church and just as I usually do, I got into the car to read some of the paper before heading off to church. I always look at your weekly ad, but that Sunday your full-page Easter message showed up first. I was so touched at the raw life-giving message, I started to cry.

There goes the mascara and all the rest! I'm tearing up now just thinking about remembering it. Your message was so bold and pure and to the point. Thank you for being so outspoken for the truth. I told my husband later when I showed him the Easter Message, "That's why I like spending my money at Hobby Lobby!" And boy, do I!

So, now more than ever, I will pick Hobby Lobby to help support a company that shares our love for our Savior. God bless you all...and don't stop those messages!

PS: Next Easter I'm reading the paper *before* I put on my makeup.

Dear Mr. Green:

In a time when Christians are told we can't pray, can't read the Bible, can't mention Christ's name, can't talk openly about Christianity because we may offend someone, it is *great* to open the papers and see your ad. Thank you for having the commitment to help spread God's message. The world would be better if there were more like you. God bless you and your family.

. . .

Dear Mr. Green:

Hobby Lobby is new to my community. I am happy to have you in our neighborhood! I thank you for standing up for our precious Christian heritage. This nation was founded on those principles and God has blessed our nation with freedom. May God richly bless your business and honor you as a man with conviction for the things of God. I admire and respect that in a business today. May God richly bless you as you celebrate His coming again!

. . .

Dear Mr. Green:

I have been saving Hobby Lobby coupons out of the Sunday paper for my wife for many years. She loves to shop there and I myself have purchased a few older military airplane models.

I did not know anything about your advertising in papers across the country about our Savior, Jesus Christ, until I received news about it today. I certainly will support your stores even more now that I know you do this. How could I have missed your ads?

I remember once at the checkout I mentioned purchasing "dope" for my model. Besides indicating advanced age (we called small bottles of paint "dope" when I was a kid), I seemed to shock your young lady that was checking us out. After we got everything settled, she promised not to call the police!

Dear Hobby Lobby:

God bless you guys for (a) leveraging your recognizable name to point people to God, and (b) risking the backlash that could come from this kind of thing. In a world where people can be sued for putting nativity scenes in their yard but get federal funding for blasphemous art projects, this takes bravery. I'm sure there has been/will be some negativity sent, but God will bless you, regardless.

. . .

Dear Hobby Lobby,

Thank you for your continued commitment to keeping Christ in the forefront of your business when all other businesses attempt to conform to the politically correct. Ironically, being politically correct today is not what it would have been when this country was founded. Without God, there would be no United States of America, but that's not how everyone sees it. It's sad to see how, in my fifty years of life, that this Country's moral values have deteriorated, and how religion, and God, have been suppressed and removed from every aspect of life.

. . .

Dear Hobby Lobby:

I am very proud of Hobby Lobby for standing up for Jesus Christ and sending holiday messages on the Internet. Not only that, but for forgetting about how much money you could bring in on Sundays and giving your employees a day off to attend church or be with their families. That alone gives a testimony to customers that you are a Christian organization. I don't know of very many large firms that would do what you are doing. I love Hobby Lobby and being a frequent customer, I know the employees at your store by their first names. I have never had a bad experience at the store. The people are very friendly and cooperative and exemplifying what Christianity is all about. Thank you for what you do. Many times you might think you are not noticed as far as these things go, but you are in my book! Keep up the good work.

. . .

Dear Hobby Lobby,

I will keep this short and simple—this message was *exactly* what I needed this morning. Thank you and keep up the good work!

. . .

Dear Hobby Lobby:

The world has gotten very hard for people to live in right now. People feel as if they have nowhere to turn. Thank you for placing these ads and making people remember that God is always walking beside them and is there to carry them, if needed. He gave us His Son to cleanse our souls. How much more can He do to show us how much He loves us. You touched my heart with all your ads, the one from Easter 2009 made me cry. God bless all of you for doing these ads.

. . .

Dear Friends,

Wow, I just went to your Web site to see if you had your usual 40% off coupon today, and saw the front page. I was totally floored. That is so cool. I knew you were a Christian company, but have never seen anything like this on your Web site before. I am a Christian and am struggling through some stuff this week, and seeing this, it almost felt like God just wrapped His arms around me, and reminded me that He is always with me, even when I don't feel it. So *thanks* for being God's messenger today! It made a big difference in my life!

. . .

Dear Hobby Lobby,

Thank you so much for your continued stand for solid Christian values. I make it a point to shop at your store for the craft needs because I appreciate the calm background music, the helpful staff, and the store cleanliness that all obviously come from the solid management style. Please continue to display a positive image and stand for Christ in the current anti-Christian times.

This final letter is so powerful due to the second letter that accompanied it.

•   •   •

Hobby Lobby Stores
To the President:

I purchase items quite often at our Hobby Lobby store here in Sioux Falls, SD. I love it. The employees are great.

I wanted to write you and applaud you for having the store closed on Sunday. I think that makes a wonderful statement in today's retail world.

I'm especially blessed by your full-page ads at Christmas and at Easter. I guess ad is the wrong word. It's really a witness to a needy world. Your agency is very perceptive and does a wonderful job in the message the page sends. It is very refreshing and uplifting.

I pray God's blessing on your business. I would encourage you to continue your witness in our community.

The following letter accompanied the letter above.

I apologize for the delay in the mailing of this letter [the preceding one]. But, you see, this was the last written piece that my husband produced. He died so very unexpectedly and quickly a few hours later. Our family has been very blessed by your witness, as well. The children wanted copies of the letter, so thus, the delay. •

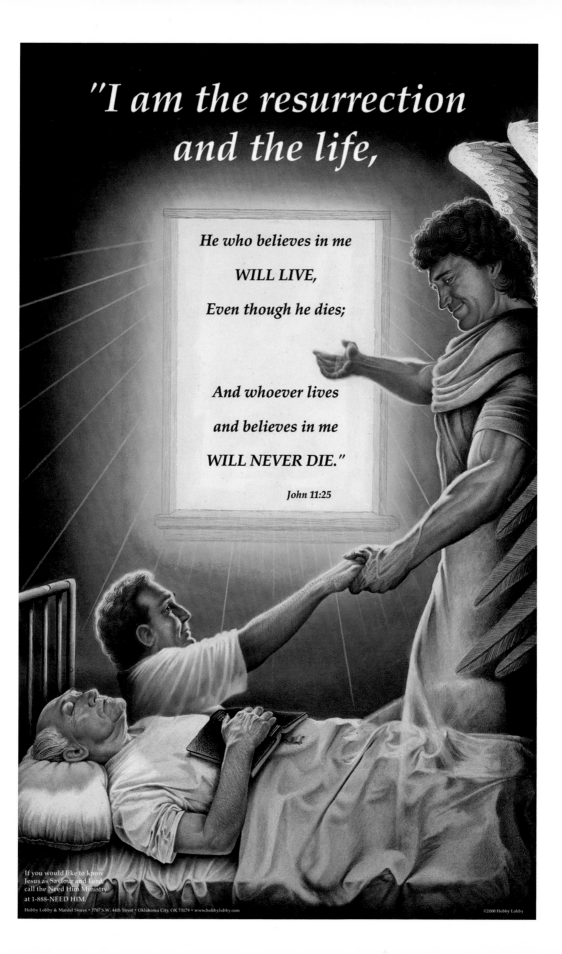

NOTES

1. David Green with Dean Merrill, *More than a Hobby: How a $600 Start Up Became America's Home and Craft Superstore* (Nashville: Thomas Nelson, 2005), 159–60.

2. Christian Overman and Don Johnson, *Making the Connection: How to Put Biblical Worldview Integration into Practice* (Puyallap, WA: Biblical Worldview Institute, 2003), 14.

3. Overman and Johnson, *Making the Connection,* 14, 16.

4. David A. Noebel, *Understanding the Times: The Collision of Today's Competing Worldviews* (Manitou Springs, CO: Summit Press, 2008), 15–16.

5. W. Gary Phillips, William E. Brown, and John Stonestreet, *Making Sense of Your World: A Biblical Worldview* (Salem, WI: Sheffield Publishing, 2008), 16.

6. Josh McDowell, *The New Evidence That Demands a Verdict: Evidence I and II* (Nashville: Thomas Nelson, 1999), x–xi.

7. Catholic News Agency Web site, February 17, 2010, www. catholicnewsagency.com.

8. Noah Webster, *History of the United States* (New Haven: Durrie & Peck, 1832), 339.

9. Daniel Webster, *Mr. Webster's Speech in Defense of the Christian Ministry and in Favor of the Religious Instruction of the Young. Delivered in the Supreme Court of*

the United States, February 10, 1844, in the case of Stephen Girard's Will (Washington DC: Gales and Seaton, 1844), 52.

10. Thomas Jefferson to Joseph Jones, August 14, 1787, in *The Works of Thomas Jefferson,* ed. Paul Leicester Ford, 12 vols. (New York: Putnam, 1904), 5:332.

11. *Annals of Congress,* 8th Cong., 2nd sess., 78.

12. Thomas Jefferson to Rev. Samuel Miller, January 23, 1808, in *Memoir, Correspondence, and Miscellanies, From the Papers of Thomas Jefferson,* ed. Thomas Jefferson Randolph, 4 vols. (Boston: Gray and Bowen, 1830), 4:103–4.

13. David J. Brewer, *The United States: A Christian Nation* (1905; repr., Atlanta: American Vision, 1996), 13.

14. Brewer, *United States,* 40.

15. Noah Webster, "Reply to a Letter of David McClure on the Subject of on the Proper Course of Study in the Girard College, Philadelphia, New Haven," October 25, 1836, in Noah Webster, *A Collection of Papers on Political, Literary, and Moral Subjects* (New York: Webster and Clark, 1843), 292.

16. Noah Webster, *History of the United States* (New Haven, CT: Durrie and Peck, 1832), p. 6.

17. Joseph Gales, ed., *The Debates and Proceedings in the Congress of the United States,* 42 vols. (Washington DC: Gales and Seaton, 1834–56), 1:27.

18. John Adams to Thomas Jefferson, June 28, 1813, in *The Works of John Adams, Second President of the United States,* ed. Charles Francis Adams, 10 vols. (Boston: Little, Brown and Co., 1850–56), 10:45–46.

19. Thomas Jefferson, *The Papers of Thomas Jefferson,* ed. Julian P. Boyd et al., 33 vols. (Princeton: Princeton University Press, 2008).

20. James Madison, Proclamation for a Day of Thanksgiving, March 4, 1815, from an original letter in the possession of David Barton.

21. *Acts Passed at the First Session of the Fifth Congress of the United States of America* (Philadelphia: William Ross, 1797), 43–44.

22. John Adams to Thomas Jefferson, April 19, 1817, in *Works of John Adams,* 10:254.

23. Thomas Jefferson to John Adams, May 5, 1817, in *Memoir, Correspondence, and Miscellanies,* 4:301.

24. Webster, *Mr. Webster's Speech in Defense of the Christian Ministry*, 27.

25. *Abington School District v. Schempp,* 374 U.S. 312, quoting *Murdock v. Pennsylvania* 319 U.S. 105, 111 (1943).

26. Harry S. Truman, "Exchange of Messages with Pope Pius XII," August 28, 1947, The American Presidency Project, http://www.presidency.ucsb.edu/ws /?pid=12746.

27. Ronald Reagan, "Proclamation 5018: Year of the Bible, February 3, 1983, The American Presidency Project, http://www.presidency.ucsb.edu/ws /?pid=40728.

28. Mike Riddle, *The New Answers Book 2,* ed. Ken Ham (Green Forest, AR: Master Books, 2008), 206.

29. Richard Dawkins, *The God Delusion* (Boston: Houghton Mifflin, 2006), 147.

30. Georgia Purdom, *The New Answers Book 1,* ed. Ken Ham (Green Forest, AR: Master Books, 2006), 277–78.

31. Purdom, *New Answers Book 1,* 280–81.

32. Much of this material comes from an interview with Kamal Saleem recorded on a DVD entitled *In the Red Chair: Kamal Saleem* (Coldwater Media, 2007). For the sake of authenticity, many violent details of Kamal's story are left unedited on the DVD, so viewer discretion is advised. See also Saleem's book, *The Blood of Lambs: A Former Terrorist's Memoir of Death and Redemption.*

33. For a more detailed look at this story, my brother Mart has produced two films that are now on DVD that give added insight. *Beyond the Gates of Splendor* is a documentary and *The End of the Spear* is a feature-length film.

Much of this section comes from material gleaned from both of these excellent productions.

34. Much of the material in this section is gleaned from the DVD *Miss HIV* (Ethnographic Media, 2008).

35. Alexis de Tocqueville, *Democracy in America,* 2 vols. 1:304.

36. De Tocqueville, *Democracy in America,* 1:304–5.

37. De Tocqueville, *Democracy in America,* 1:308.

38. De Tocqueville, *Democracy in America,* 1:309–10.

39. De Tocqueville, *Democracy in America,* 1:310.

40. De Tocqueville, *Democracy in America,* 1:311

41. De Tocqueville, *Democracy in America,* 1:311–12.

42. Alexis de Tocqueville, *The Republic of the United States of America and Its Political Institutions, Reviewed and Examined,* trans. Henry Reeves (Garden City, NY: A. S. Barnes, 1851), 1:337.

43. De Tocqueville, *Democracy in America,* 2:6–7.

44. Herbert Casson, *Cyrus Hall McCormick: His Life and Work* (Chicago: A. C. McClurg, 1909).

45. Casson, *McCormick,* 25.

46. Stephen McDowell, *Building Godly Nations* (Charlottesville, VA: Providence Foundation, 2004), 255.

47. McDowell, *Building Godly Nations,* 263.

48. McDowell, *Building Godly Nations,* 265.

49. Joseph H. Appel, *The Business Biography of John Wanamaker, Founder and Builder* (New York: Macmillan, 1930).

50. Appel, *Wanamaker,* xv.

51. Appel, *Wanamaker,* 16–17.

52. Appel, *Wanamaker,* 50–51.

53. McDowell, *Building Godly Nations,* 14–15.

54. Appel, *Wanamaker,* 194.

55. Appel, *Wanamaker,* 205–6.

56. Appel, *Wanamaker,* 208.

57. Appel, *Wanamaker,* 437.

58. Appel, *Wanamaker,* 322–23.

59. Appel, *Wanamaker,* 340.

60. Appel, *Wanamaker,* 280–81.

61. Appel, *Wanamaker,* 224.

62. Benjamin Rush, *Essay Literacy, Moral and Philosophical* (Philadelphia: Thomas and William Bradford, 1798).

63. Much of the material in this section comes from an excellent DVD produced by David Barton titled *Four Centuries of American Education* (Wallbuilders, 2004).

64. Massachusetts, *The Laws and Liberties of Massachusetts: Reprinted from the Copy of the 1648 Edition in the Henry E. Huntington Library* (Cambridge: Harvard University Press, 1929).

65. *Engel v. Vitale,* 370 U.S. 421 (1962) (Justice Potter Stewart, dissenting).

66. Foundation for Individual Rights in Education, *Spotlight on Speech Codes 2011: The State of Free Speech on Our Nation's Campuses,* http://thefire.org /public/pdfs/312bde37d07b913b47b63e275a5713f4

67. Adapted from James Allan Francis, *The Real Jesus and Other Sermons* (Philadelphia: Judson Press, 1926), 123–24.